Harry Roberts and Foxtrot One-One
The Shepherd's Bush Massacre

Geoffrey Barton

Foreword Mike Waldren QPM

☆ WATERSIDE PRESS

The Shepherd's Bush Massacre 1966

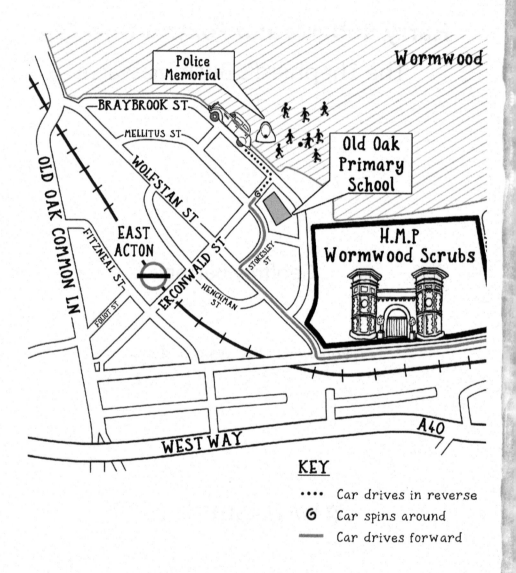

Map of the area showing getaway route

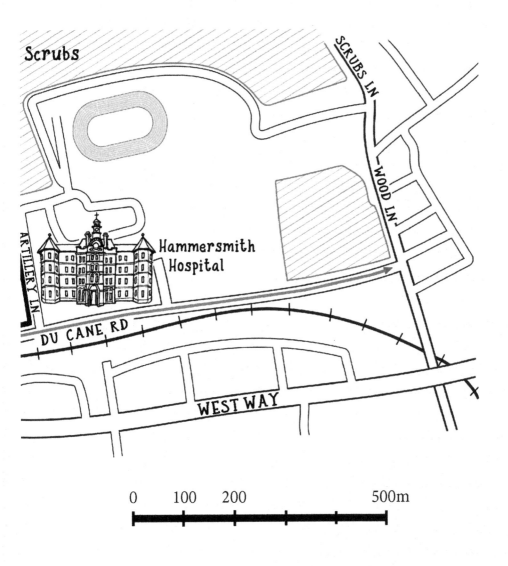

Drawn by Lydia Bevan at Hand Drawn Maps, Herne, Kent

Harry Roberts and Foxtrot One-One: The Shepherd's Bush Massacre
Geoffrey Barton

ISBN 978-1-909976-47-4 (Paperback)
ISBN 978-1-910979-45-7 (Epub E-book)
ISBN 978-1-910979-46-4 (Adobe E-book)

Cover design © 2017 Waterside Press by www.gibgob.com Based on artwork by Heidi Kuivaniemi-Smith: see *About the cover artist*.

Printed by Lightning Source.

Main UK distributor Gardners Books, 1 Whittle Drive, Eastbourne, East Sussex, BN23 6QH. Tel: +44 (0)1323 521777; sales@gardners.com; www.gardners.com

North American distribution Ingram Book Company, One Ingram Blvd, La Vergne, TN 37086, USA. Tel: (+1) 615 793 5000; inquiry@ingramcontent.com

Cataloguing-In-Publication Data A catalogue record for this book can be obtained from the British Library.

e-book *Harry Roberts and Foxtrot One-One: The Shepherd's Bush Massacre* is available as an ebook and also to subscribers of Ebrary, Ebsco, Myilibrary and Dawsonera.

Published 2017 by
Waterside Press Ltd
Sherfield Gables
Sherfield on Loddon, Hook
Hampshire RG27 0JG.

Telephone +44(0)1256 882250
Online catalogue WatersidePress.co.uk
Email enquiries@watersidepress.co.uk

Table of Contents

The Shepherd's Bush Massacre 1966   *ii*

Copyright and publications details   *iv*

About the author   *ix*

The author of the Foreword   *ix*

Acknowledgements   *x*

Cover images   *xi*

About the cover artist   *xii*

Foreword...*xiii*

Introduction... 15

1   **The Murders**... 19

So What Happened?   *20*

Why Was the Standard Vanguard in Braybrook Street?   *22*

Why Did the Detectives 'Stop' the Vehicle?   *24*

Earlier in the Day ...   *25*

Back on Patrol   *27*

Dreadful News for Det Insp Coote   *28*

Getting to Grips with What Happened   *28*

Informing the Officers' Families   *29*

The Inquest   *33*

The Funeral of the Officers   *34*

Memorial Service   *35*

Background and Issues   *38*

2   **The Victims**... 45

Temporary Detective Constable David Wombwell   *48*

Police Constable Geoffrey Fox   *49*

3 The Area: F District 53

The Prison and the Hospital *56*

4 The Detectives 57

Head of the CID *57*

Head of the Murder Squad *58*

Head of the Flying Squad *58*

Senior Investigating Officer *58*

Investigating Officer *61*

The Forensic Scientist *62*

The Ace Thief-Taker *62*

Another Detective *64*

The Officer in Charge of Q-Cars on F-Division *64*

The Inside Team *65*

Home Office Pathologist *66*

5 The Investigation 67

Tracing the Owner of the Standard Vanguard *68*

Tracing the Vehicle *73*

Proving Witney Parked the Vanguard in the Garage *75*

Charging Witney *77*

Catching Duddy *78*

The Search for Harry Roberts *83*

Roberts' Women *84*

The Arrest of Harry Roberts *86*

Roberts' Life in the Woods *89*

The 'Fund-Raising Party' *93*

Tracing the Source of the Guns *96*

6 John Witney and John Duddy 103

John Edward Witney *103*

John Duddy *105*

7 Harry Roberts: This Is Your Life 107

Expansion of the Parole System *123*

Abolition of Capital Punishment   *123*

8   **The Women in Harry Roberts' Life** 127
        Mrs Dorothy Roberts: Harry's mother   *128*
        Lilian Perry and June Howard   *133*

9   **So Why Braybrook Street?** 139
        A Short History of Wormwood Scrubs Prison   *140*
        Harry Roberts in Wormwood Scrubs   *142*
        John Witney and John Duddy   *143*
        George Blake   *144*

10   **The Trial** 147
        The Appeals   *164*

11   **Imprisonment For Life (Prisoner 231191)** 165
        Parole   *170*

12   **Roberts' Release** 177
        John Duddy   *177*
        John Witney   *177*
        The Final Release Decisions   *183*
        Reaction to Harry Roberts' Release   *184*
        The police   *186*
        Politicians   *187*
        The trial judge   *188*
        The latest woman in Roberts life   *189*

13   **Epilogue: Meeting Harry Roberts** 191
        Conclusion   *194*

Index   *195*

List of Illustrations

Map of the area showing getaway route   *ii*

Top: Detective Sergeant Christopher Head, Temporary Detective Constable David Wombwell, Police Constable Geoffrey Fox   *xi*

Bottom: Harry Roberts, John ('Jack') Witney and John Duddy   *xi*

The murder scene in Braybrook Street, Shepherd's Bush soon after the shootings   *19*

A Standard Vanguard estate car of the type used by the police killers   *23*

Police Memorial Trust commemorative stone next to Braybrook Street   *43*

Left to right: Police Constable Geoffrey Fox, Temporary Detective Constable David Wombwell, Detective Sergeant Christopher Head   *45*

The Standard Vanguard estate getaway vehicle discovered by the police in Lambeth, south-London before the killers were able to remove and dispose of it   *74*

Front page of the *Daily Mirror* indicative of the mass coverage by the media of what remains the biggest and most intense manhunt in British criminal history   *83*

Roberts' hideaway in Thorley Wood, Hertfordshire expertly constructed using camouflage and survival skills gained in the British Army   *87*

Sergeant Peter Smith, left, and Sergeant Oswald Thorne   *89*

Reward poster   *95*

The guns used by the killers   *99*

'Have you seen this man?' Metropolitan Police Service handout, 1966   *107*

The crowded crime scene in Braybrook Street within the police cordon as the investigation began   *139*

The Wombwell family. Gillian Wombwell with her late husband, David and their son Daen   *184*

About the author

Geoffrey Barton is a skilled and experienced thief taker. After joining the Metropolitan Police Service in 1975, he learnt his trade in Brixton and Walworth, where his size, strength and power soon singled him out as a fearsome adversary. He focused on professional street criminals, pickpockets, muggers and armed robbers. Having become a well-known and noticeable character on the streets of south London, he took to sitting in observation posts, identifying suspects to teams of surveillance officers who then followed them until they were about to commit or committed offences and were arrested. He was selected for firearms training and focused on tackling dangerous robbers and murderers including serial killers. He regularly arrested as many as ten suspects a day and on three occasions more than 50 in 24 hours.

The author of the Foreword

Mike Waldren QPM (1947–2017) was Historian to the Police Firearms Officers Association. A chief superintendent with the Metropolitan Police Service, he was Head of MPS Firearms Training and Operations. After 33 years in the police, he retired in 2000 but was still consulted by those in authority, including government ministers and chief constables, who relied on his knowledge and experience as a consultant.

Acknowledgements

I would like to express my appreciation to Paul Bickley and all those at the Metropolitan Police Crime Museum (formerly known as the Black Museum), for their assistance and support in this project. The future of the museum is unclear at this time, as the Metropolitan Police Service (MPS) moves to a new headquarters on the Victoria Embankment later this year. May the new Metropolitan Police Commissioner, Cressida Dick, and her colleagues realise the real value that the museum provides to the service and find room for it in the new building.

I am also grateful to Lee Tribe at the Office of the Mayor of London, for allowing me to view the exhibits in the case, held in the Metropolitan Police Crime Museum at New Scotland Yard.

Phillip Barnes-Warden and his colleagues at the Metropolitan Police Heritage Centre at the Empress State Building in Barons Court gave me valuable assistance in tracing the exhibits and documents in the case. For that I am grateful.

Finally, to late-Chief Superintendent Mike Waldren QPM who, as a consequence of the very incident recorded in this book, was selected for the newly-formed Metropolitan Police Firearms Branch and took advantage of the opportunity to set down policy relating to the use of firearms by both the MPS and the entire British Police Service for the next half century. Regrettably, Mike died on 28 December 2016. His obituary appeared in the *Guardian* newspaper of Saturday 4 March 2017.

Geoffrey Barton
July 2017

About the cover artist

Heidi Kuivaniemi-Smith is a Forensic Artist based in Buckinghamshire who specialises in facial identification and is involved in research in the field of investigative interviewing. Her interests lie mainly in the fact that facial distinction can provide a lead for police investigations. She also undertakes commissions for portraits, working in pencil and grey-scale pastels, as well, for example, as photo restoration work and digital art. 'Inspired by the human face', Heidi is creating a project Faces of the World: see further www.facialdepiction.com

Key to drawing on the previous page

Top: Detective Sergeant Christopher Head, Temporary Detective Constable David Wombwell, Police Constable Geoffrey Fox.

Bottom: Harry Roberts, John ('Jack') Witney and John Duddy.

Foreword

The public execution of three police officers in a quiet suburban street, in front of a large number of young children playing football, provoked considerable public outrage in 1966. Two of the suspects were quickly arrested, but the third, Harry Roberts, escaped into Epping Forest and hid there.

There are many stories about the armed searches to find Roberts, including that of an officer, who had only Army experience to call on, being given a Webley revolver in a cardboard box. After being given a box of ammunition he was told: 'Don't you load it whatever you do, but most importantly don't you bloody well use it on anybody. You just go out there and arrest this bloke and then bring that thing back to me and I'll put it away'.

Home Secretary Roy Jenkins was asked in Parliament, 'In what circumstances is he now authorising the arming of the police, uniformed and in plain clothes; and what consideration has he given to a general extension of the present authority'. He replied, 'Arms are available for issue to police officers who are on protection duty or need to carry them for self-defence when engaged on specially dangerous duty, and who have been trained to handle them. I do not contemplate any substantial change in these arrangements, but I am considering, in consultation with the organizations representing the various ranks in the police service, a number of detailed improvements, for example, in firearm training'.

As always, the Police Service adapted to face the armed criminals with which it had to deal. The Metropolitan Police Firearms Unit was established and continues until today.

Geoffrey Barton has made a careful study of the event and the story is told with commitment. More than that, his book goes into considerable detail about the participants, the social conditions of the time and the aftermath. It is clear that in the absence of an armed response in the way that it is structured by police forces today, the officers involved did their best relying on guts and determination to see them through an unprecedented incident.

Mike Waldren QPM

Introduction

In a police career spanning 25 years I have served with the Metropolitan Police Flying Squad, the Anti-Terrorist Branch and the Met's initial firearms response team. I have been involved in more than 500 face-to-face confrontations with men (and occasionally women) carrying loaded firearms. I have faced twice as many people who *claimed* to be armed, but who, fortunately, were not. On occasions I have been required to take action that I have had to justify to both coroners and senior officers, in order to save innocent lives.

What follows is the true story of one of the most notorious crimes in modern English legal history. Known as the Shepherd's Bush Murders (or Massacre of Braybrook Street) they involved the shooting dead of three police officers on 12 August 1966. The officers, on routine patrol, opted to question three men, Harry Roberts, John Duddy and John Witney, who were sitting in a Standard Vanguard estate car parked in the shadow of Wormwood Scrubs Prison. Almost immediately, Roberts shot dead Temporary Detective Constable (TDC) David Wombwell and Detective Sergeant Christopher Head, following which Duddy shot and killed Police Constable Geoffrey Fox. All three culprits fled the scene but were later arrested (Roberts after famously going to ground in woodlands and one of the most high profile and longest police searches of all time). All three men were tried, convicted and sentenced to life imprisonment. This book is about these tragic events, their social context, the long-term effect on the victims' families, their impact on UK policing, the use of police firearms and the twists and turns in the case as the years passed.

I do not really blame Duddy and Witney for what they did in Braybrook Street; they had little alternative. If they had attempted to stop Roberts, they would have found themselves facing an extremely dangerous man, armed with at least one firearm and they would probably themselves have died if they had attempted to restrain him in any way.

They would then have needed to summon the police and give themselves and give up their 'prisoner' Roberts to them, in order for all three to face trial, and the reality of facing the rest of their lives in prison. The skill is to avoid getting yourself into the situation in which these men found themselves.

I do, however, blame all three, Roberts, Duddy and Witney, for taking firearms out with them when committing their crimes. That is where they deserve to be punished. Let the government recognise this and put out a clear message to anyone thinking of taking weapons out onto the streets. Let there be *no* exceptions, whoever these people are. The message will soon get around and criminals will soon realise that it is not worth carrying arms when committing crimes.

Harry Roberts accepts these facts. In 2004, having served almost 40 years for the murder of three detectives, he told the media, 'I accept if you carry a gun that you know that at some time you will have to use it'. But as I explain at the end of the book, and though he has been released, I believe he still lacks remorse. While Roberts was strenuously pushing for parole he said, 'When I returned to Britain, I took up my old life as a criminal. I teamed up with Witney and we did dozens of armed robberies together ... on betting shops, post offices ... The most I earned was £1,000 from a single job. Witney was the eldest, the boss: he knew the best places to rob. Duddy joined us later'. But it is more likely that the gang had committed hundreds of robberies rather than dozens. And Roberts carefully avoided mentioning all the old men working as rent collectors that the gang had robbed.

When he was 18-years-old Roberts was told, upon being convicted of smashing a heavy glass decanter over the head of a 78-year-old victim and cutting off his finger in order to steal his wedding ring, that he had missed 'the rope' by the narrowest of margins. Wandering around London committing hundreds of armed robberies, it was always just going to be a matter of time before one of their victims resisted or they were stopped by the police.

The following chant is sung to the tune of *London Bridge is Falling Down*. It originated with groups of young people outside Shepherd's Bush

Police Station after Roberts had been arrested and is now still sometimes sung by football supporters to taunt police officers.

Harry Roberts is our friend,
Is our friend,
Is our friend.
Harry Roberts is our friend,
He kills coppers.

Let him out to kill some more,
Kill some more,
Kill some more,
Let him out to kill some more,
Harry Roberts.

He shot three down in Shepherd's Bush,
Shepherd's Bush,
Shepherd's Bush,
He shot three down in Shepherd's Bush,
Our mate Harry.

Another chant is where Roberts' name is shouted repeatedly: 'Harry Roberts, Harry Roberts, Roberts Roberts, Harry Harry' in a parody of the Hare Krishna mantra, 'Hare Krishna, hare Krishna, Krishna Krishna, hare hare'.

But, 50 years in an eleven feet by six feet cell as a Category-A prisoner, with only prison warders for company, awaits anybody who wants to emulate their 'hero' ...

CHAPTER 1

The Murders

Friday 12 August 1966 was a hot and peaceful summer's day; all was well with the world in Braybrook Street in Shepherd's Bush, west-London. Just 13 days earlier, and four miles down the road at the old Wembley Stadium, the entire population of the country had united to support the England soccer team as it beat West Germany 4–2 to win the World Cup, and the country was still basking in the reflected glory.

The murder scene in Braybrook Street, Shepherd's
Bush soon after the shootings

At around 3.15 pm the silence was broken when Geoff Fox drove a Triumph 2000 saloon index number GGW 87C down the road with a couple of pals: Chris Head was in the front passenger seat and Dave Wombwell in the back. On their right they passed Wormwood Scrubs, the scrubland with all its football pitches; on the left they passed rows of 1930s houses which made up the Old Oak Common Housing Estate. Many of these were occupied by the families of prison officers working at nearby Wormwood Scrubs Prison, the high walls of which were 100 metres behind them.

Local residents later reported seeing the Triumph come up behind a Standard Vanguard estate car index number PGT 726, parked at the side of Braybrook Street, outside number 61, with three men inside. As the Triumph stopped, Head and Wombwell got out and walked over to the Standard and spoke to the driver through his car window. Suddenly, and without warning, the front seat passenger bent forward, reached down deep into an old holdall at his feet, pulled out a German Luger pistol and shot Wombwell through his left eye, killing him instantly. Head ran back towards the Triumph, but the gunman gave chase and aimed two shots at his back. The first shot missed, but the second hit him in the head, fatally wounding him.

Fox then attempted to drive away. Seeing this, the passenger in the rear of the Standard got out and ran towards the Triumph as Fox struggled to turn it around. Snatching a .38 Webley service revolver from the holdall, he shot Fox three times. As Fox died, his foot hit the accelerator and he drove over the dying body of his pal, Chris Head. The two gunmen then raced back to the Standard and the driver, unable to deal with seeing the bodies lying in the road, reversed off at speed, but not before his vehicle registration number had been taken down by a witness. Two minutes afterwards the silence had been broken it was replaced by a deathly hush ...

So What Happened?

With the football pitches of Wormwood Scrubs on one side, houses occupied in the middle of the day only by busy housewives on the other, and the only business in the area being the Old Oak Primary School, most of the witnesses were young children. Some of them ran home to tell their mothers what they had seen.

This group of women and children were stunned by what had just happened. They struggled to piece together the events from the information they had, and considered what they needed to do next. Mothers called their children and took them indoors where they would be safer, and calls were made via the 999 system to the information room at New Scotland Yard. The information was circulated to patrolling radio cars, instructing them to attend the scene to investigate, and also to take all due care in order to avoid any further deaths. As everybody who knew anything about the incident waited for more information and struggled to understand what had just happened and why, there was a hush across London. All this happened in a very short space of time:

3.15 pm	The occupants of the two cars meet for the first time;
3.17 pm	The shooting occurs;
3.19 pm	The first call reporting the incident is received at New Scotland Yard;
3.20 pm	Deputy Assistant Commissioner Mullen assigns Detective Superintendent Chitty to investigate the incident.

The first officers to arrive at the scene of the massacre were from Shepherd's Bush and Hammersmith Police Stations. They quickly recognised the Triumph 2000 as a 'Q-car', a police car manned by local detectives and managed by the local Criminal Investigation Department (CID) (and see the explanation later in this chapter). A cursory examination of the scene confirmed their worst fears: the dead men were Detective Sergeant Christopher Tippett Head, aged 30; Temporary Detective Constable David Bertram Wombwell, aged 25; and Police Constable Geoffrey Roger Fox, aged 41. All were attached to Shepherd's Bush Police Station. Word quickly spread and more resources were directed to the scene: senior officers, detectives, forensic medical examiners, forensic scientists and many other specialists.

The first car to arrive at the scene was driven by PC Sidney Seager. PC Seager had met his wife at Geoff Fox's family home; he had been best man at his wedding. Two days later, in an unrelated incident, he was on traffic duty and was killed when an articulated lorry overturned and ran him over.

It is now nearly 200 years since the formation of the Metropolitan Police Service (as it is now known) and in that time there have been four occasions in which three police officers have been murdered; this was the first for half a century and it would be almost another 20 years before the next: the Harrods bombing of 1984. Needless to say, such an incident prompts fierce emotions and decisive action.

There can be no doubt that as the three occupants of the Standard Vanguard estate drove away, they did so very carefully, at 29 miles per hour. They would not want to be stopped by one of the thousands of police officers who had been told to look out for them. At some stage, these three men would have needed to pull over, talk about what had just happened, and discuss what to do next. Finally, they would have wanted to dump the car, split up, and go away to deal with their own shock and anxiety. Years later, the leader of the killers told an author that a few minutes later a police motorcyclist looked as if he was going to stop them as they left the scene and he seriously considered killing him too.

Friends and relatives who saw the three men that evening spoke of them sitting alone, in silence. They would have been trying to come to terms with what they had done, and thinking what they must do now, and what the future held for them. Over the next couple of hours, many of the most senior Scotland Yard detectives visited the scene. One of the first CID officers to arrive was newly-promoted Detective Inspector Jack Slipper from the Flying Squad at New Scotland Yard. He had been patrolling the area in an unmarked Rover when the incident occurred. For the last three years he had been one of the six officers investigating the Great Train Robbery that occurred on 6 August 1963.

Why Was the Standard Vanguard in Braybrook Street?

The three occupants later admitted that they had been working as armed robbers, picking on soft targets: old men working as rent collectors; off-track turf accountants (that were now permitted under recent legislation); post offices and small banks and building societies. Realising that the Vanguard was about to fall apart, they had decided to steal a replacement and had spent the day driving around in the vicinity of London Underground stations in west London looking for one. They decided that they wanted a blue Ford Cortina and had copied the number plates of one like that they had seen in the area, JJJ 285D. They intended to attach these plates to the stolen vehicle in order to confuse the police.

Having found nothing suitable around East Acton Underground Station, they decided that, as commuters would soon be returning to collect their cars, they would have to stop their activities in order to avoid detection. They decided to turn into Braybrook Street because it was so quiet and they wanted to talk about what to do next. The detectives now leading the investigation, seeing it was such a quiet area, decided that the killers could only have been there for one purpose: to assist a convict to escape from Wormwood Scrubs, possibly the man who had recently received the longest sentence of imprisonment in history, the Russian spy, George Blake. Only six weeks earlier an attempt to free Blake had been foiled, so it was not impossible that in that intervening period another plot had been hatched.

A Standard Vanguard estate car of the type used by the police killers.
An image of the actual vehicle PGT 746 appears in *Chapter 5*,
'The Investigation'. Image created by Simon GP Geoghegan.

Why Did the Detectives 'Stop' the Vehicle?

Foxtrot One-One was a crime car, focused on high-level crime work. At 3.10 pm, Det Sgt Head had responded to a call from his boss, Det Insp Coote, asking to be picked up from Marylebone Magistrates' Court with a box of bulky exhibits. It would take at least 20 minutes to get to the court and even longer as it was approaching the Friday evening rush hour. The court was due to close soon after 4 pm. On their way, they obviously saw something that compelled them to stop and investigate. There are several possible reasons:

1. The Vanguard had no road fund licence. In the days when discs for display on taxed vehicles existed this frequently indicated that there were other problems, such as no MOT test certificate, no insurance, or even occasionally that the car had been stolen. If a police crew are really bored then they might use this as an excuse to stop a vehicle; but in this case their boss was expecting to be picked up so that he could have a quick getaway for the weekend, and it is unlikely they would have wasted their time.

2. The Vanguard was in poor condition. The silencer was 'blowing' and held on with string. PC Fox, as a uniformed officer, may have noticed that, but if the officers intended to prosecute the driver in respect of a breach of construction and use regulations they would have had to call a traffic patrol officer to the scene to examine the vehicle as an expert witness, and that would have taken an hour or two.

3. It has been said that PC Fox once lived a few doors down from the man later shown to be the driver of the Vanguard. Perhaps he recognised his former neighbour and knew of his criminal proclivities. The driver was not in fact a professional criminal, but neither was he a saint.

4. The Vanguard was less than 100 metres from the walls of Wormwood Scrubs. It may have been closer when the detectives first saw it. Det Insp Coote was prosecuting five men for a prison break a few months earlier; attempts to break out were relatively frequent. Indeed, when news of the shootings spread to the prison, it was put into lock-down and a serious potential escaper was put under

special measures to ensure his safety and security. Did talking to the DI put the seed of suspicion in the minds of the detectives?

5. Seeing three men in a car is always suspicious. It is common to see a couple in a car, or adults and children, or even two men in a car; but seeing three or four men in a car often means that it is either a police car, such as Foxtrot One-One, or a gang out to commit crime. Perhaps they just gave out the wrong vibes and that is why the detectives stopped to have a look and a 'little chat'.

6. If the detectives had caught sight of the false number plates they were carrying (see earlier in this chapter), that would certainly have caught their attention.

Earlier in the Day ...

So what had happened that day to bring together the two teams who met up at 3.15 pm in Braybrook Street with such terrible consequences?

Foxtrot One-One

Q-car crews are the best thief-takers in the best cars, with the best drivers, taking the best calls. On F-Division in 1966 the crews worked either an early turn (9 am to 5 pm) or a late turn (6 pm to 2 am) The officers would have invariably arrived at the police station to start work between 8.15 am and 8.30 am.

As a detective sergeant usually working in the CID Office, Chris Head had a considerable caseload awaiting trial at the Old Bailey, the Inner London Crown Court, or the local West London Magistrates' Court. There would be solicitors and barristers needing to speak to him and discuss his cases. He would have a call list to work through every time he got near to a telephone. As the driver, Geoffrey Fox was responsible for the maintenance of his vehicle. Before taking it out onto the road he would have a 30 point check to complete, covering all the fluid levels, the performance of every system on the vehicle, and the tyre pressures. If he detected a fault that he did not feel qualified to repair, then he would have to arrange to visit the local workshop in order to exchange the vehicle.

The first priority on early turn would be to fill up the petrol tank; afternoons and evenings can get very busy, and at that time most of the garages closed at night, so early turn was the best chance you got. Few vehicles are driven 24 hours a day, seven days of the week, but Q-cars often are, and it takes its toll. The MPS does not employ mechanics, it employs fitters. This means that every car resembles Trigger's Broom on *Only Fools and Horses*: 'I have used the same broom for 20 years. It has had 17 new heads and 14 new handles!' A Q-car could be only a year old, but it might have had three new engines, four new gear boxes, and six new sets of brakes!

The success or failure of a Q-car crew is determined largely by the junior detective. Temporary Detective Constable (TDC) Dave Wombwell would have been constantly tapping his contacts in both the CID office and among the uniform officers, to secure information that was of use to the crew in securing arrests and the recovery of stolen property.

Det Insp Coote, as a CID officer, started work at 9 am. He was due at court at 10 am and expected to be there all day, so he would have arranged to meet the crew of Foxtrot One-One at 9 am in order to give them their daily briefing, as it would be the only opportunity that he would get to meet them if he was detained at court all day. The car would have to leave Shepherd's Bush Police Station no later than 9.20 am if they were to be confident of arriving at court by 10 am, and questions would be asked Coote was late! The car would, therefore, have been on regular patrol between 10.30 am and 1 pm. There is no record of where they went or what they did between those hours on that day. The radio operator, TDC Wombwell was required to maintain a log of all the calls that he made or received but, in a fast-moving vehicle, this frequently became untidy and officers often kept notes on scraps of paper and updated the log in a quiet moment later in the day.

At around 1 pm Foxtrot One-One returned to Shepherd's Bush Police Station for the officers to take their meal break. Chris Head and Dave Wombwell would probably have quickly checked their messages and made any urgent telephone calls, while Geoff Fox would have used the car radio to show the car as being 'off watch' with information room.

Then the three policemen walked the 400 metres along Uxbridge Road to Shepherd's Bush Common and the *Beaumont Arms* (now the *Defector's Weld*) at 170 Uxbridge Road, Shepherd's Bush, on the corner with Wood Lane, where they went for lunch most days when they were working nine-to-five. They chatted with the landlord, Fred Brounfield and his blond wife Joyce, and placed their order for lunch, talking about football, particularly their team, Chelsea. When their meals arrived they had to eat them quickly and finish their drinks before rushing back to the station to get back on patrol. In the days before mobile telephones it was essential to keep in touch, so Head and Wombwell would have again checked for any messages before they all got back into the car, and then Chris Head got back on the radio to show the car as 'back in the green' or back on watch. This message was timed at 1.57 pm.

Back on Patrol

Foxtrot One-One was a patrol vehicle, so they had nowhere in particular to go other than the usual crime hotspots or to follow up on any information that they had received. They drove along Shepherd's Bush, past the now defunct BBC Television Centre in Wood Lane and the White City Stadium, famous for hosting the athletics for the 1948 Olympic Games, but in 1966 a popular venue for greyhound racing. At 3 pm a radio call went out from the Information Room for Foxtrot One-One to contact their boss, Detective Inspector Coote at the gaolers' office at Marylebone Magistrates' Court. His case was over and he wanted to arrange a lift back to Shepherd's Bush Police Station with his three tea chests of exhibits. At this time, Det Sgt Head and TDC Wombwell were out of the car following a man pushing a pedal cycle down the road, who they felt was suspicious, so PC Fox acknowledged the message.

A couple of minutes later the two detectives had dispelled their suspicions — either they had spoken to the man or he had done something which satisfied them that the bicycle was his own — and they got back in the car. PC Fox passed on the message from Det Insp Coote and they went looking for a telephone box, there being no mobile telephones or personal radios in those days (as opposed to the innovation of radio cars and their operators as in the case of Foxtrot One-One). When they found a telephone box, Head got out, called Coote at the court, and arranged to pick him up. It was then 3.10 pm; the magistrates tended to rise at 4 pm, when there is a dash for the door, especially on a Friday. Something must have caught the crew's attention, because instead of heading straight for the court, they drove down Braybrook Street, a quiet cul-de-sac at the back of Wormwood Scrubs. What came next has already been described earlier in the chapter.

Dreadful News for Det Insp Coote

By 4 pm Det Insp Kenneth Coote was no longer patiently puffing his pipe as he stood beside his stack of exhibits waiting to be picked up. Far from being pleased, he rang the station and snarled, 'Where the bloody hell's my transport?'

'Haven't you heard, sir?'

'Heard what?'

'The crew of Foxtrot One-One have all been killed'.

'How?' he asked, thinking there must have been a collision on the way from Acton. 'Was there an accident?'

'No sir. They were shot'.

'Right. Obviously you'll need all the transport you've got. Don't worry about me. I'll get back as best I can'.

He rang Paddington Police Station, where they knew what had happened. They told him, 'We'll send Sergeant Miller with his car. You've got him for as long as you want'.

Miller found Coote stunned. 'Three wiped out at one hit!' he kept saying. 'What the hell can have happened? They were doing a normal, run-of-the-mill job'.

Getting to Grips with What Happened

Not knowing what had happened or what they were dealing with, the first police officers to arrive at the scene had a difficult task on their hands. They spoke to all the available witnesses. Most of them were young children who had been playing football on The Scrubs. Arrangements were made for the scene to be sealed off to prevent members of the public from trampling all over the evidence or walking away with any of it. Photographers were called to take pictures from every angle. Forensic scientists collected and documented any scraps they could find.

No doubt local contingency plans were consulted in order to identify suitable ones to implement.

A police surgeon would have been called to the scene to confirm that the officers were dead. In 1966 only a doctor could certify life extinct, even in the most obvious cases, such as a decapitation. In a case as serious as this, the Home Office pathologist would be called to the scene to conduct a preliminary investigation. When this had all been completed and the photographs and forensic examination were complete the bodies of the three officers would have been removed to the mortuary pending post mortem examinations at the first opportunity. The initial suspicions were that the incident had been related to the presence of the nearby prison and a potential escape attempt. The prison governor was contacted and arrangements made to secure the prison as much as possible. All prisoners were returned to their cells and the most dangerous ones transferred to alternative prisons.

At the same time, senior detectives met up both at the scene and at Shepherd's Bush Police Station to decide what had happened, who was going to be doing what in the investigation and what needed to be done as a priority. Reports would need to be submitted to the Assistant Commissioner, the Commissioner, the Home Secretary and Prime Minister. Clearly, somebody would have to talk to the media.

Informing the Officers' Families

While the murderers were making good their escape, the police were identifying the deceased and making arrangements to inform their families. No amount of training can ever prepare anybody for sitting down with a person and breaking it to him or her that their spouse has died and that their family's life has fallen apart. When the death is violent and unexpected the task only gets harder; when the officer has no answers for their questions it is as hard as it can get.

The person selected to inform the families of the dead officers was the station welfare representative, Detective Constable Alastair Dent. He was an ex-heavyweight boxing champion of the Royal Air Force, who was known locally as the 'gentle giant'. He was telephoned at his home — to which he had just returned to celebrate his birthday, after working early turn from 6 am to 2 pm.

'You'd better come back,' he was told. 'Three of our lads have been shot'.

'Who?'

'Not sure yet'.

Dent had driven back to the station in his old car, found everyone too stunned to talk, and had gone to the communications room to find out what exactly had happened. Having learned the facts, and having ensured that someone in Torquay would visit Mrs Head, he prepared to visit the two widows.

Though he was good at his job—helped by his obvious sympathy for anyone bereaved and by his comforting resemblance to John Wayne—he hated it. F-Division had for too long been known as the murder area, and with each of its murders—not to mention its traffic fatalities and suicides—Dent seemed to have inherited the unenviable task of breaking the news to the victim's mother, or wife or family. It never got any easier, it always terrified him, and it still depressed him. But none of the ordeals of the past compared with this one. Not only had the dead men been his brother officers and friends, Dent also knew how pitifully inadequate would be the pensions on which Mrs Wombwell and Mrs Fox would henceforth, with their children, have to survive.

Phyllis Head

At 4 pm Christopher Head's white-haired mother, Mrs Phyllis Hilda Head, was taking tea with a neighbour in Barewell Road, St Mary Church, Torquay, Devon, 212 miles west, and a four-hour drive, away from Shepherd's Bush. They were listening to a concert on the radio when the music was interrupted by a news flash announcing that three policemen had been shot. Mrs Head was not a nervous woman, but she confessed later that on hearing this news she had a sudden, awful premonition that her son had been involved in the incident. 'It was like a cold finger touching my heart,' she recalled. 'I tried to tell myself I was silly, and tried to go on drinking my tea, but the feeling persisted. I could no longer hear the music'.

Unsettled by the news, she made her way back home. She had gathered her two young grandchildren to her when the front doorbell rang. The door was opened by her eldest son, and a uniformed police sergeant entered the house. The sergeant stood in the hall while he gently broke the news to him. Upon hearing it, Head went to his mother and sent the two children to play in the garden. 'I knew from his face what had happened,' she said. 'I suppose I had known from the time I heard the news on the radio'.

It was not the first time that tragedy had touched the Head family. Mrs Head had been widowed when Christopher was only five-years-old. At that time, she had lived with her husband, who worked at the Royal Naval College, and four children, in a council house in Dartmouth. After the death of her husband, it had been a struggle for her, but she had brought her children up well. Christopher, a quiet lad, had been born on Christmas Eve in 1935 in the local hospital at Dartmouth. He went to the local school and passed the eleven-plus examination to get a place in the grammar school.

Margaret Fox

As the oldest man in the crew, PC Geoffrey Fox had been married for nearly 19 years and had two teenage children and a young baby. Mrs Margaret Fox was preparing tea for their two-year-old daughter, Mandy, at their council flat near Yeading Green, Northolt, Middlesex, ten miles from Wormwood Scrubs, when she heard the news. Their 18-year-old daughter Ann was working as a secretary at the time and their 16-year-old son, Paul, was a technician at a photographic laboratory.

Like Mrs Head, Mrs Fox had also previously had to deal with tragedy, when she was orphaned by the death of her mother at the age of 14 and had to bring up a family of younger brothers and sisters. At that time, Mrs Fox had been living near the scene of the murders, in Braybrook Street and, as a child, had often played on Scrubs Common.

Shortly after the shootings, Mrs Fox felt unable to stay in a home that constantly reminded her of her husband and their life together, and moved away. 'I always knew my Geoff would get killed some day,' she said, 'but he always wanted to be a policemen, and was proud of his job, as so was I, of his job, and him'. 'I just want to stay in the background,' she said, 'but as a policeman's wife, who knows nothing about politics and that, I think it is wrong that criminals should be glamorised. So many of them seem to get so little when they do go to court, and some of them get away altogether'.

Gillian Wombwell

Mrs Gillian Wombwell, a slim, graceful 21-year-old with deep blue eyes, was in the block of flats at East Acton, where they lived close to Wormwood Scrubs, when the news of her husband's death came. Their son, Daen, aged three, was playing with his aunt in the garden. Their daughter, Melanie, celebrated her second birthday at her father's funeral. Mrs Wombwell paid tribute to her neighbours: 'I just want to say how wonderful everyone has been,' she said, 'My neighbours have scrubbed floors, done my dusting and shown me what they feel in so many ways that mean so very much to a woman'. Upon hearing the news, she asked the officers to inform her husband's mother, Daphne van der Scoot, who had divorced his father and was now married to Mr Ben van der Scoot. Together, they kept a storybook country pub in Melbourn, Cambridgeshire. On 12 August the garden was beautiful with trees in blossom and the song of the birds gave an added tranquillity to the quiet summer's day.

Later this white-haired mother talked about the day she heard her son was dead. Frequently bursting into tears, she said, 'Ben, my husband and I were choosing wallpaper for the kitchen, when the phone rang that Friday afternoon. We argued, jokingly, about who should answer it, because we were so wrapped up in our decorating plans. In the end I went. A man asked for my husband and wouldn't say who he was. Then I heard my daughter-in-law, Gillian, trying to say something and crying, and the man came on again and asked for my husband'.

'Ben came to the phone and I listened in. It was the police, and Gillian was with them, and they told us what had happened. When Ben came off the phone, he put his arm round me and led me back to the kitchen. I slumped down into a chair, and I kept saying, "It isn't true. It can't be. This kind of thing only happens to other people." We were slightly dazed. Ben took it as hard as I did. He loved (David) like his own. We had to open up that evening, but I couldn't face it. I went to a friend up the road, and she poured me a huge scotch. I'm not a drinker, but I didn't even feel it. I was just numb. The customers were marvellous to Ben. A stranger even offered to wash up—everybody wanted to help'.

The Inquest

The office of HM Coroner is an ancient one, dating back at least to 1194. Its duties and responsibilities are covered by the Coroners Act 1988. The coroner is assisted by officers, who may be civilians or police officers. The main duty of a coroner is to enquire into sudden or unexplained deaths, usually by holding a post-mortem inquiry, followed by an inquest if the cause of death is not natural. Hammersmith and Fulham was the lead authority of the West London Consortium which consisted of six boroughs' coroners' services. Coroners' officers are employed by the police, whilst the coroner is a local authority appointment. Their main duties include arranging post mortems, holding of inquests to find the cause of death and issuing certificates for burial or cremation.

On Monday 15 August the inquest on the three detectives was opened at Hammersmith Coroner's Court by Cyril Baron, the West London Coroner. He said, 'This was an appalling and dreadful crime which has resulted in the deaths of three courageous police officers, officers who have been killed in the execution of their duty. They were officers whom the police and the public could ill afford to lose'. Only police and reporters were present at the brief hearing and evidence of identification was given by Det Insp Coote. The coroner asked Detective Superintendent Chitty how his investigation was progressing and its current position. Chitty told him that one man had been charged and would be appearing at West London Magistrates' Court in connection with the killing of the officers. He added, 'Two other men are being sought'. Before Chitty left the witness box, Baron said, 'I am sure that the public are deeply grateful to you and the other officers who have been investigating this case, for what I am sure have been the very long hours, and the tireless efforts you have put into it. Thank you'. Slightly embarrassed by the praise and the gratitude, Chitty replied, 'We have only done what was expected of us'.

The Funeral of the Officers

It was just 20 days after the incident in Braybrook Street, on Thursday 1 September 1966, and just a mile away, that the three policemen were slowly borne in their coffins through the sympathetic silence of the crowds who lined the roads of Shepherd's Bush, uncomplaining in the rain and wind. Stationed at strategic points were armed detectives, just in case Roberts decided to return—only a vague possibility, but not one to be ignored.

The people were five deep in front of the shops, most of which had been closed for the duration of the service at the rather plain Victorian Gothic Church of St Stephen and St Thomas in the Uxbridge Road, opposite the station where the three men worked in the CID office on the second floor. On the roof of the station, the Union Jack was at half mast, and down the road many flags flew with black pommels on the flag staffs. More than 600 uniformed policemen stood along the kerb at four metre intervals, just as they do on state occasions or on demonstrations when they might be required to keep order in a hostile crowd. But there was no hostility that day, only a solemn, almost unmoving crowd.

At 10 am the church bell tolled and, at the same time, a lament was played by a single piper in the courtyard at Scotland Yard, where a simple 15 minute service was held for officers who had to remain on duty. Fourteen funeral cars moved slowly along Uxbridge Road to the church and at 10.15 am the relatives walked up the aisle. It was a grief stricken procession, where women wept. Sir Joseph Simpson spoke to the mourners and then took his place in a pew with Deputy Commander John du Rose of the CID. Around them the church was packed with officers from all over London, many of them from the station across the road. And there were local civilians, councillors, shopkeepers, street traders, publicans and the Mayor of Hammersmith, Councillor Leonard Freeman.

The police officers who bore the coffins on their shoulders expressed most poignantly the feeling of that morning; six to each coffin, each pair joined with arms behind their backs; detectives for the two detectives, Christopher Head and David Wombwell, and uniformed officers for Geoffrey Fox. A young uniformed officer from the local station, PC

Bernard Horan, read the lesson, from the fifteenth chapter of the First Epistle to the Corinthians.

The service was conducted by the vicar, the Reverend John Ashbridge, and among the congregation was the archimandrite of St Nicholas Orthodox Greek Church, Panteleimon Coulouris, representing the Cypriot population of Shepherd's Bush. Hymns were sung, including *Abide with Me* and *On the Resurrection Morning*, and the MPS choir sang two voluntaries. Dispassionately, the Order of Service described the dead as 'police officers killed whilst on duty' and the Suffragan Bishop of Kensington, the Right Reverend Ronald Goodchild, said in his sermon that everybody there, both inside and outside the church, was there to offer homage to 'three brave men'. The bishop said that the people had come to say, 'Thank you'. They had come to think not of all the publicity which had, not unnaturally, been attracted to their deaths, but to 'think of one of the fundamental truths of our society which this tragedy has brought home to us. It is a stern reminder of what we really ask of our policemen'. He added that we live in a society in which we all belong to one another. The welfare state emphasises the responsibility we have for each other as it seeks to provide for our just needs and our proper security. 'Let us pause and think that what we ask of our policemen is not only the maintenance of law and order so that our freedoms may be protected—we ask for the protection of our lives, if need be at the cost of their own. It is a great deal to ask and we are sharply reminded of it in this tragedy'.

Among the hundreds of people who sent flowers was Mrs Harry Roberts—gold and white chrysanthemums—who had not seen her wanted husband for seven years and who was working as a striptease dancer in the north of England. It bore a card which said, 'With deepest sympathy. Mrs Margaret Roberts, Jnr'. The police officers were taken away to Chiswick Cemetery, Staveley Road, London, where Head and Fox were buried and Wombwell cremated. Slowly the crowds dispersed.

Memorial Service

The day of the memorial service was as sunny as the day of the murders, and it was the supreme tribute to the three men who fell in the constant and dangerous battle against crime. Long before noon, when the service began, the approaches to Westminster Abbey were jammed with ordinary people who, because they had no tickets for the church, were content to stay outside sitting on camp stools or folded-up newspapers. And then came the long, steady marching lines of policemen and policewomen, from all the forces in Britain. There were 2,000 of them, from all the senior officers to the raw recruits, their badges gleaming, their faces grim

Donald Zec, a journalist, wrote of the day:

'The setting is as familiar as it is famous ... for the celebrated, the excited, the royal, the warriors of rank and doers of great deeds. But these magnificent yet immensely moving proceedings had no touch of ermine, no jangle of spurs. Just police helmets and sergeants' stripes; blue serge and heavy boots; and the ceremonial armament with the uniforms was no more lethal than the whistle and truncheon. This I suppose is the antique significance of it all. A random trio from London's police force suddenly and tragically projected into history. One day just three names on a roster at Shepherd's Bush; yesterday, in highly distinguished company, those names on a roll of honour. Two wives and a mother in the Abbey made suddenly and painfully conspicuous.'

Zec continued by describing how everyone sensed the feelings of the assembled police officers, serving and retired. He noted how the steps of the widows of Geoffrey Fox and David Wombwell and mother of Christopher Head seemed to strengthen as they entered Westminster Abbey, and as they saw vast ranks of 'men in blue'. Prime Minister Harold Wilson, and Leader of the Opposition Edward Heath, were present along with other senior politicians, including Roy Jenkins, the a then Home Secretary, who has a special responsibility for policing throughout England and Wales. The Metropolitan Police Band played solemn music. There were men in top hats and black frock coats, dignitaries with gold chains, noble lords and traffic wardens, barristers, magistrates and judges, young nurses, baronets and civil servants. But the overwhelming impression was of a field of dark blue and silver, of stern faces, old and young. Her Majesty Queen Elizabeth II was represented by Lord

Hilton of Upton (who in a strange twist was stopped and asked for his ticket on security grounds as he made towards the entrance. He waited patiently as enquiries were made, before he was admitted).

As the long procession of clergy, police and prison chaplains and others, moved into the abbey, the congregation sang *Guide Me, Oh Thou Great Redeemer*, with a crescendo at 'Death of death, and hell's destruction, land me safe on Canaan's side'. Sir Joseph Simpson KBE, Metropolitan Police Commissioner, read the lesson from the *Book of Revelation*, xxi, 1–7:

'And I saw a new heaven and a new earth: for the first heaven and the first earth were passed away; and there was no more sea. And I John saw the holy city, new Jerusalem, coming down from God out of heaven, prepared as a bride adorned for her husband. And I heard a great voice out of heaven saying, Behold, the tabernacle of God is with men, and he will dwell with them, and they shall be his people, and God himself shall be with them, and be their God. And God shall wipe away all tears from their eyes; and there shall be no more death, neither sorrow, nor crying, neither shall there be any more pain: for the former things are passed away. And he that sat upon the throne said, "Behold, I make all things new". And he said unto me, "Write: for these words are true and faithful". And he said unto me, "It is done. I am Alpha and Omega, the beginning and the end. I will give unto him that is athirst of the fountain of the water of life freely. He that overcometh shall inherit all things; and I will be his God, and he shall be my son".'

The congregation followed the choir in singing *The Lord's My Shepherd*, and next the Dean said, 'I ask you, whether here or at home, to search your own heart. May not these killings, which have so shocked us, along with the hard realities by which our nation is faced at the present time, mark a turning point in our society in a general revulsion against brutality and in a determination that our society shall not slide into violence?"

The Dean then commended to God, Christopher Tippett Head, Geoffrey Roger Fox and David Stanley Bertram Wombwell, 'whose death came suddenly to join them in the course of their duty as servants of the law and order of our land'. They sang *Abide With Me* and there were prayers for the mourners, especially for the families of the victims.

The service ended with the Metropolitan Police choir singing, unaccompanied, *God Be in My Head* when many a hardened policeman cried without embarrassment. A collection was taken in aid of the Police Dependants' Fund. A crowd of about 1,000 had gathered outside the Great West Door, among them about a dozen carrying banners calling for the restoration of capital punishment for the murder of police and prison officers; to coincide with the service, signatures were collected in Whitehall. The service had been relayed to St Margaret's, the church next door to the abbey which is employed as an overflow for major events. It was packed with policemen and public, as were cathedrals and churches elsewhere throughout the country. It was at St Margaret's, as reported in *The Times*, that a uniformed inspector from the provinces, said gruffly to a long lost friend, 'I thought they gave us a very nice show'.

Anybody who picked up a newspaper could then have read about another incident the previous night in south London, where 150 youths attacked three detectives and tried to drag an arrested man out of a police car. The battle was fought outside a café, where the man was arrested, on the outskirts of south London. Some of the youths jumped onto the roof of the police car, others dragged opened the doors and grabbed the prisoner. They almost hauled him clear but the detectives hung on and fought off their attackers. The crowd then tried to overturn the police car, but the detectives managed to drive away back to the police station.

Background and Issues

Q-cars

A Q-car is an emergency response vehicle, staffed and managed by the CID. It is responsible for patrolling an entire district of the MPS, roughly the same as a London Borough, and an area usually covered by about four police stations. The name 'Q-car' derives from 'Q-boat', as operated by the Royal Navy during the First World War. Tatty old boats were fitted with exceptionally large engines and even bigger guns. The Germans, believing that they were approaching an old wreck, relaxed until they were alongside it, whereupon the 'old wreck' suddenly opened fire and sent the German vessel to the depths of the ocean. The boats were exceptionally successful, as were the police cars.

The Metropolitan Police fitted brand new, highly-tuned, four and five litre V8 engines to ancient Wolseley, Morris and Austin saloons and put the best crime fighters, ace detectives and thief-takers in them, with an unlimited overtime budget. The results were spectacular.

The driver was a Class 1 police driver, a police constable, who usually drove the uniformed radio/telephone (R/T) cars in uniform. Being a prime posting and step towards the ultimate job, driving for the Flying Squad, the role was highly coveted and only the best, most pro-active officers needed to apply. As the radio had never to be left unattended, the driver stayed in his seat for the entire shift, leaving the two detectives to speak to suspects, buy refreshments and liaise with colleagues and managers. The radio operator and 'writer' for the car was usually a young, explosive, plain clothes officer with ambitions to join the CID: the 'engine' of the crew, seeking information, warrants and tips with which to keep the arrests coming in, scouring the horizon for possible 'stops' (suspects to stop or search), then writing up all necessary reports.

The observer, as in all police vehicles, was the senior officer. Usually a detective sergeant. He was the 'brains' of the operation; a senior man, the older man, expected to be the person to introduce a little judgement and moderation to the job. He would try to show that he 'still had it' and could still find the best jobs, either by getting the highest quality information, or targeting the most fruitful 'stops', whilst still having to maintain his existing caseload by responding to urgent enquiries from the Attorney-General (A-G), Director of Public Prosecutions (DPP) and (what is nowadays) the Crown Prosecution Service (CPS) as well as defence solicitors.

Police use of firearms

In 1966 the police were extremely reluctant to resort to the use of firearms, even when facing the most dire threats. When the Metropolitan Police was formed in 1829 officers were issued with long truncheons, while stocks of pistols and cutlasses were held at police stations. After the Second World War, the police started to 'believe their own press', and that their strength was in not carrying weapons but being able to talk to the public. Whilst, these are great strengths, there would always be people who were committed to the use of violence, even terminal violence, as Harry Roberts showed, and who need to be confronted with superior firepower.[1]

As a police officer who has had to use firearms against criminals whilst on duty, I am outraged that even after the men in Braybrook Street had shot and killed three police officers for almost no reason at all, the MPS sent their men in to arrest the suspects without firearms, not just once, but several times. Nowadays, quite rightly, a senior officer taking this decision could face action for both personal and corporate compensation for damages, even if no officer was injured.

Body armour

Only in 1980 did the MPS purchase its first sets of body armour. They were allocated to Ranger 500s, the first MPS vehicles to carry permanently armed police. I was the operator of Ranger 500 on the day that the body armour was purchased and was summoned to Great Scotland Yard to collect it. A couple of hours later we were sent to an incident in Tottenham Court Road Underground Station and I got to tear off the plastic bags in which they had been supplied and issue the armour to my colleagues to wear in an armed confrontation. I remember that it felt very heavy and restricted our movement considerably. The public were totally taken aback to see police officers wearing body armour and openly carrying firearms at that time.

---

1. One curiosity in the wake of the Braybrook Street Massacre (and sent two days afterwards) is a letter from Field Marshall The Viscount Montgomery of Alamein KG, GCB, DSO: 'From Isington Mill, Alton, Hants. 14-8-66…My Dear Simpson, I am horrified by what went on in the Wormwood Scrubs area on last Friday. In 1953 I was presented with a revolver in a handsome case by the Turkish Army, Turkey having joined NATO in 1952. It is a MKE Kirrikkale 9mm, together with 50 rounds of ammunition. The Prime Minister, Winston Churchill, approved of my accepting the gift. It has been kept locked in my safe ever since. A few weeks ago I came across it, having forgotten about it, and had it overhauled and fired by the armourer sgt of the Depot, the Parachute Regt, Aldershot. He reported it to be in perfect condition. I would now like to present it to the Metropolitan Police for use in seeking out armed murderers or for any use you wish. Will you accept it? Yours sincerely, Montgomery of Alamein'. The letter is now on display in Scotland Yard's Police Museum (formerly the Black Museum).

Ten years later, in 1990, body armour was issued to every police officer required to operate outside a police station and shortly after that, to every traffic warden and community support officer. Unfortunately, in 1966, although any police sergeant could issue firearms without deferring to a senior officer, they were seldom in fact issued and officers frequently approached armed suspects, even those known to be ready to use violence, without the protection that weapons provide.

Radio communications

In 1966 the MPS fitted all R/T cars, vans and unmarked general purpose cars with force radios. But personal radios were a thing of the future and it would be another six years before they were issued to every patrolling officer, allowing them to respond to calls more quickly and to call for assistance when threatened.

Interestingly, there were police boxes, and there was one close to Braybrook Street; but officers would have to know the location of a nearby box, find it, unlock it, call the station and wait for someone at the station to answer, before they got any assistance.

In 1966, as today, police officers were aware that their communications were being monitored, and moderated their messages. I joined the MPS in 1975 and was informed that certain words and phrases that were not permitted on police frequencies: 'guns' 'pistols', 'rifles', 'ammunition' and 'bullets', were all banned, as were any similar words. Instead, officers referred to 'equipment'. There were other euphemisms used in police communications. For example, sexual offences were never referred to on the radio. Instead, the terms, 'serious offence' or 'arrestable offence' or later 'serious arrestable offence' were used. It is interesting that, although the three officers were shot and killed instantly, the radio messages broadcast after the incident referred to 'GBH' (grievous bodily harm).

Police Dependants' Trust

After the murders, the deceased officers' young families received the following:

- Det Sgt Head's family a gratuity of £362;
- TDC Wombwell's family a pension of £7 6s 0d a month;

• PC Fox's family a pension of £9 16s 3d a month.

The Police Service has always been cautious about the acceptance of gratuities from members of the public, whether they are made to the service as a whole, or to individual officers. Although there is an obvious risk that police action could be affected by such gratuities, when these are accurately recorded, openly published and freely discussed, and where simple guidelines are established, this caution should be unnecessary. In 1966 this caution initially resulted in senior police officers ordering that all donations, whether cash or goods, to the deceased officers, be declined.

This generated conflict between the police and the public who were outraged at the cold-blooded murder of their local police officers and who wanted to show their respect to them and their support for the officers' families. Senior officers were forced to relent and arrange for police officers to accept and record all donations. Eventually a total of £210,000 was raised by the collection, with 12.5 per cent, or £26,500, being presented to the closest surviving relative of each of the deceased officers. The remainder was put in trust for their children. The initial conflict later resulted in the creation of the Police Dependants' Trust, which was established to accept, record and monitor donations to the families of deceased police officers. Their website declares:

> 'So great was the public outrage [after the Braybrook Street Massacre] that a donation of £100,000 from the late holiday camp pioneer Mr (later Sir) Billy Butlin soon swelled to more than £1 million. The Police Dependants' Trust was up and running…Regrettably, officers still lose their lives in the line of duty, while others sustain serious injuries, the effects of which can, and often do, bring disaster to the officers and their families for the rest of their lives. And it's not just the headline-making events that take their toll on the police. Hundreds of equally harrowing, but less high profile stories are held in the Trust's files.'

The families of many former police officers, as well as some who are still serving, have credited their present quality of life to the support they have received from the trust. So far it has supported some 7,000 beneficiaries and distributed grants totalling more than £45 million.

Police Memorial Trust

This trust was founded by Sir Michael Winner in 1984 and placed a permanent memorial to the three detectives in Braybrook Street, near the site of their murders, in 1988.

Police Memorial Trust commemorative stone next to Braybrook Street

CHAPTER 2

The Victims

Left to right: Police Constable Geoffrey Fox, Temporary Detective
Constable David Wombwell, Detective Sergeant Christopher Head

Detective Sergeant Christopher Head

Christopher Tippett Head joined the police service as cadet in Torquay,
Devon when he was 17 years-of-age, soon after leaving school. He
threw himself enthusiastically into his new career and began to learn
the workings of the police service and his role within it. He soon became
well-known, walking around the town in his smartly pressed uniform
with its peaked cap.

Head served as a police cadet for 18 months until he was 19, at which
age he was no longer eligible to be a police cadet, but was eligible to join
the police as a constable. During his time in Torquay he gained a good
general insight into criminal investigation, traffic law and the many and

varied problems which beset the man in the street and with which police officers are called upon to deal.

In 1952 it was compulsory for every young man aged 19 years to perform National Service in one of the armed forces, either the Army, Royal Navy or Royal Air Force. Due to his service as a police cadet, Head was sent to the Royal Air Force and posted to the RAF Police, stationed in Stranraer in Scotland. Upon completing his two years' National Service, Head was demobilised and returned home to Dartmouth. He applied to join the Railway police and passed the police entry examination and the Selection Board, but was rejected on medical grounds, when the doctors decided that he was colour-blind.

Devastated at this decision and aware that all forces impose similar conditions of entry, Chris took alternative employment as a metal polishing inspector at an aircraft factory at Newton Abbey and put aside all thoughts of joining the police. However, after 18 restless months, aware that his colour-blindness was borderline, he decided to try again, and applied to the Metropolitan Police.

Metropolitan Police Central Record of Service

Christopher Tippett HEAD

Warrant number:	51/146521
National Insurance Number:	ZM/86/24/68/D
Born:	24/12/35 in Dartmouth, Devon
Joined Metropolitan police:	23/6/58
Height:	5'10.5"
Marital status:	Single
Education:	Grammar School
Former trade or calling:	The Metal Polishing Inspector
Former police service:	Cadet Devon Constabulary 1/9/52 to 16/3/54
Former military service:	RAF Police 24/3/54 to 6/6/56

Date	District	Borough	Promoted to
23/6/58	TS	Training School	PC
29/9/58	B	Kensington & Chelsea	
13/5/63	F	Hammersmith & Fulham	DC
10/2/64	COC10	Stolen Car Squad	
19/10/64	C	Westminster	
1/4/65	E	Camden	
25/10/65	COC1	Major Crime Squad	
28/2/66	F	Hammersmith & Fulham	DS
12/8/66	Died	Service 8 years 1m 21 days	

Next of kin

Mrs Phyllis Hilda Head (mother)

In June 1958, he became PC Head and joined the Metropolitan Police training school at Peel House, in Regency Street in Westminster. His superiors found him quiet and unassuming, but very determined, and he passed the course well, displaying a natural aptitude for study. Even when he went home to Torquay, where his mother now lived, for the occasional weekend, his mother would find him lying in bed in the mornings with his nose in the instruction book, the policeman's bible. And always on Sundays, at home, he would go to St Luke's Church, where he had once helped with the youth club and acted as a sidesman.

His training completed, he was posted to Fulham Police Station in September 1958, and grew to love the area. He got on well with the local people and was particularly popular with the street traders in North End Road market. Some of them found difficulty in coping with business correspondence and the young police constable used to write letters for them in his off duty time. Those same people were useful to him when he worked in plain clothes as an aid to CID, giving him little titbits of useful information; an invaluable service to any policeman.

When he was appointed to the CID after six years' service, he went to Scotland Yard's central office, where all the major criminal investigations are handled, and while he was there he passed the examination for sergeant. A brief spell with the Stolen Car Squad followed, under Detective Superintendent Jack Knight, and on promotion to sergeant, he was sent to Shepherd's Bush, adjacent to Fulham, the area of London that he knew and liked best. At the time of his death, he was 30 years of age.

Temporary Detective Constable David Wombwell

In the back seat of the Triumph Q-car was the youngest man in the crew, David Stanley Bertram Wombwell, who was 27 and had joined the Metropolitan Police in February 1963. He was born in Weston Way, Baldock, Hertfordshire and attended the primary school there. While he was young his parents separated and David was brought up by his father, Kenneth Wombwell, and his grandmother, Mrs Ethel Wombwell, who was 84 at the time of David's death.

David Wombwell went to two other schools, first in Bedford, and then at Broadmead School in Tennyson Road, Luton, after which he took a course in motor engineering at the Luton School of Technology. One of his first jobs was with Chater-Lea, the motor engineers of Letchworth, Hertfordshire, but he had always been keen on a police career and he applied to join the Hertfordshire Constabulary cadet force; but at the time, there were no vacancies.

When his father moved to Harpenden, David entered the employment of the Electric Hose and Rubber Company, which made high-pressure hoses used in mines and submarines. For two years he was the personal driver to Don Taylor, the managing director. Within a few hours of the murders, Taylor had written a tribute to David's personality and character, which was published in the local press.

Metropolitan Police Central Record of Service

David Stanley Bertram WOMBWELL

Warrant Number:	34/152227
National Insurance:	ZX/08/70/87/B
Born:	16/4/41 Baldock, Herts

Joined Metropolitan Police: 23/6/58

Height: 5'10.5"

Marital status: Married

Education: Technical education

Former trade or calling: Trainee car salesman

Former police service: None

Former military service: RAF Police 24/3/54 to 6/6/56

Date	District	Borough	Promoted to
10/2/63	TS	Training School	PC
20/5/63	F	Hammersmith & Fulham	
2/1/66	F	Hammersmith & Fulham	TDC

Next of kin
Mrs Gillian Wombwell (wife)
Daen Andrew Wombwell (son, born 2/6/63)
Melanie Ann Wombwell (daughter, born 6/9/64)

Wombwell was working as a car salesman in Harpenden when he met the girl who was to become his wife, Gillian Hague. At the time, she was a hairdresser in the village and they married at St Albans Registry Office in 1962. It was a year later that he joined the Metropolitan police and three years later he became a Temporary Detective Constable. He was considered promising material, and for that reason was assigned to the Q-car, Foxtrot One-One, to gain experience. He was shot through his left eye by Harry Roberts.

Police Constable Geoffrey Fox
Driving the Q-car was 41-year-old Geoffrey Roger Fox, without doubt one of the most popular uniformed constables at Shepherd's Bush. Since he had joined the force in July 1950, he had always been at the same station and the number on his uniform collar, 107 F, was well known around the streets where he walked the beat. This man had a remarkable aptitude for nosing out crime—of being in the right place at the right time to prevent or detect, felony. It was because of this faculty that he was often in demand by the CID.

He had developed a number of extremely good contacts who gave him information on the activities of local criminals, many of whom he had arrested. His experience and knowledge of local thieves, which had gained him three commendations from the commissioner, as well as his Class 1 driver qualification, made him the ideal Q-car driver. (There are five classes of police driver. Class 1 takes six months and in 1966 cost £20,000. Only Class Is were allowed to drive Q-cars or Flying Squad cars).

Yet, although he was a dedicated man of action as a policeman, his favourite pastime was sitting by a river with a fishing rod. Sometimes he took younger policemen with him. He used to tell them that it was a good way to relax from the boredom of police duty. Some policemen believe that he once lived near John Witney, and it may be that on 12 August, he recognised him driving the battered old Vanguard. That is something which will never be known, for the knowledge died with Fox, a bullet from John Duddy's gun through his brain.

Metropolitan Police Central Record of Service

Geoffrey Roger FOX

Warrant Number:	05/135997
National Insurance:	?L?/89/51/93/D
Born:	22/12/24 Godstone, Surrey
Joined Metropolitan Police:	24/7/50
Height:	5'09"
Marital status:	Married
Education	Elementary
Former trade or calling	Bus Conductor
Former police service:	None
Former military service:	7/12/42 to 27/8/46 (National Service)

Date	District	Borough	Promoted to
24/7/50	TS	Training School	PC
6/11/50	F	Hammersmith & Fulham	
24/11/63	Class 1 Driver	Hammersmith & Fulham	

Next of kin

Mrs Margaret Fox (wife, married 29/11/47)
Ann Margaret Fox (daughter, born 29/8/48)
Paul Geoffrey Fox (son, born 30/4/50)
Mandy Ann Fox (daughter, born 3/12/63)

CHAPTER 3

The Area: F District

Roughly speaking, F District of the Metropolitan Police covers same area as the London Borough of Hammersmith and Fulham, which in 1966 had a population of about 100,000.

At the beginning of the 19th-century 5,600 people lived in Hammersmith. In 1839 (the year the Metropolitan Police was established, Thomas Faulkner, who kept a bookseller's and stationer's shop in Chelsea, wrote a history of the borough in which he described it as 'a village some four and a half miles from London, with a pleasant situation, elegant villas and a dubious reputation for its riotous support of Queen Caroline' (banished from the UK but who later returned to live here). There were many farms in the area, several around Wormwood Scrubs (previously the Anglo-Saxon 'Womholte': A dense wood which the Saxons believed to be infested with snakes!).

Hammersmith became a thoroughfare due to its suspension bridge over the River Thames designed by W Tierney Clark, the Grand Junction Canal, the Great West Road and later the Great Western Railway. This brought its own problems: thieves, footpads and highwaymen, who preyed on passing traffic. A voluntary fund was raised to give 'proper reward' for apprehending and convicting housebreakers, murderers, footpads, robbers of gardens, orchards, poultry, etc., '…as so many daring and atrocious offences have, of late, been committed'.

In 1818 a weekly subscription was collected to provide a watch patrol for the village, a move which was by then necessary due to several murders, including that of an apprentice aged eleven, and many robberies by gangs of young people. Four years before, the military built the road called Wood Lane, which now leads to Wormwood Scrubs. In the same year, a lease was taken out by the Government so that two regiments of Life Guards could exercise on the open space. Some of the land, 20 acres, was sold in 1873 to the Director of Convict Prisons, and it is on this that the gaol, built by convict labour, still stands. It was designed by Sir Edmund du Cane, the noted penal reformer, after whom 'Du Cane Road', which runs in front of the prison, was named.

This was a period of considerable development in Hammersmith. From a population in Faulkner's time of just 10,000 it had grown to over 25,000. The original police station, in the village of Brook Green, had been moved to Queen Street. The *Queen's Head*, said to have been frequented by Dick Turpin, still stands on the green near the old station, and is much patronised by policemen from Shepherd's Bush. Public houses are very much part of the backcloth of this area. The oldest now are the *Blue Anchor* in Lower Mall; *The George* in Hammersmith Broadway (once a booking office for stage-coaches) the *Hampstead Hog* in King Street (where in 1773 William Wingfield, a Heston Farmer, was robbed and murdered), the *Red Cow* and *Rose and Crown* in Hammersmith Road, and *The Sun* in Agnew Road (which was rebuilt in the 1960s after being destroyed as the result of a World War II air raid).

The *White Hart* in King Street, mentioned in the 18th-century, was used by a man called Francis Smith, who shot and killed Thomas Milwood in a nearby lane mistaking him for the 'Hammersmith Ghost'. The inquest was held in the *Black Lion*, in Black Lion Lane. Smith was tried at the Old Bailey, convicted and sentenced to hang but received a royal pardon and was released. The Hammersmith Ghost was the name given to a nocturnal figure which alarmed inhabitants by 'appearing' as a spectre. According to Faulkner, one young man, more courageous than the rest, was Francis Smith. He hid in a secluded spot, armed with a gun. When he heard approaching footsteps he shouted a challenge, and, not receiving an answer, fired. A deep groan indicated that the 'ghost' was a bricklayer, Thomas Milwood, going home late from work.

After 1945, Hammersmith began to develop as it is now. In some of the long roads the tall, many-roomed house, were converted into bedsits. A strong Irish component, which had been there for over a century, remained, but many foreigners also found their way there due to their being able to find accommodation and easy travel to work. It probably has one of the most diverse populations of any area in London, but they seem to get on well enough, each group of nationalities keeping pretty much to itself. As the population swelled, the police had to increase its numbers and improve its accommodation. F District has its chief police station at Hammersmith alongside two others, Fulham and Shepherd's Bush. It is the last of these which is at the centre of our story.

A few months before the Massacre of Braybrook Street, the MPS had closed an investigation that had been managed from 'the Bush' into a serial killer who had been active in the Hammersmith area for six years. Between 1959 and 1965 west London had been gripped by a serial killer's prostitute killing spree. A total of eight women had been found murdered in the Hammersmith area, including in neighbouring Chiswick and Brentford. The killer was never caught. The sex-worker slayings were dubbed 'The Hammersmith Nudes Murders' because each victim had been found naked except for stockings and dumped in areas around London or in the River Thames. The investigation into the killings was led by Detective Chief Superintendent (later Deputy Assistant Commissioner) John du Rose, who interviewed almost 7,000 suspects in a desperate bid to catch the culprit. Christopher Head had been one of the detectives on that investigation. The finger of suspicion for the murders was pointed at former British heavyweight boxing champion Freddie Mills, and a local security guard, Mungo Ireland, who worked on the Heron Trading Estate in Ealing, where the final victim, Bridget O'Hara, was found in 1965. When Ireland committed suicide in March 1965, under the pressure of suspicion, and Mills was found shot in the head in his car in July 1965, the police lacked any further suspects or useful leads and decided to close the investigation. That investigation had put the station in the news for many months. John du Rose had assembled a splendidly efficient team of detectives and had equipped and organized the office for the most efficient style of working. Many of the same detectives were still serving there and able to bring the same skills in the administration of a murder hunt to the Braybrook Street massacre enquiry.

The Prison and the Hospital

Wormwood Scrubs, known locally and to an extent nationally as 'The Scrubs', or simply 'Scrubs', is an open space located in the north-eastern corner of Hammersmith and Fulham. It is the largest open space there, at some 200 acres, and one of the biggest areas of common land in London. The eastern part, known as Little Wormwood Scrubs, is cut off by Scrubs Lane and the West London Line railway. Its open public space status dates from the Wormwood Scrubs Act of 1879.

The southern edge of the Scrubs is the site of two important buildings. At the western end is HM Prison Wormwood Scrubs, built between 1875 and 1891 by convict labour. 'A Short History of Wormwood Scrubs Prison' appears in *Chapter 9*. To the east of the prison is the Hammersmith Hospital campus, which includes the relocated Queen Charlotte's and Chelsea Hospital.

CHAPTER 4

The Detectives

A crime of the magnitude of the Shepherd's Bush Massacre obviously drew in some of the most senior officers in the Metropolitan Police Service, especially from the CID. Of course, the murder of serving detectives required not simply an investigation but a management and human resource response. Those present at the scene included are described below.

Head of the CID

Commander Ernie Millen, operational head of the CID, was in his office at New Scotland Yard, when, shortly after the incident, he received a call from Detective Chief Inspector John (Ginger) Hensley, in charge of the CID at Chiswick Police Station. Hensley had been the first CID officer to be informed of the incident at Shepherd's Bush and when Hensley reported the incident to him, Millen immediately appointed him second in command of the investigation.

As Millen put the phone down and started to think about who should lead the enquiry, Detective Superintendent Richard Chitty from C1 Murder Squad, and one of the brightest talents in the Metropolitan Police at the time, walked along the corridor, past his office. Millen called Chitty in and tasked him with investigating the most serious and shocking crime of the century: it was a life-changing moment. 'Three policemen have been shot in Shepherd's Bush,' Millen said bluntly, 'I want you to go down and take over'. 'But I am not on call,' began Chitty, as anyone would who had been working around the clock and was due for some rest; but then the importance of what he had been told sank in and he asked, 'Are they injured?' 'They're dead. All three,' said Millen, 'Get down to the Bush as quickly as you can. I'll see you there'.

Millen later commented:

> 'No murder ever showed the true face of crime more clearly than this shooting down of three policemen on a summer afternoon in Hammersmith. The Braybrook Street Massacre shocked the public into a realisation of the type of brutal and vicious characters that are spawned in the underworld of crime'.

Head of the Murder Squad

Commander Bill Bailey, the head of C1 Murder Squad, was Dick Chitty's boss and ultimately responsible for the investigation of all offences of murder in London.

Head of the Flying Squad

Det Ch Supt Tommy Butler, the 'Old Grey Fox', 'One Day Tommy' or, with his close friend and colleague Detective Superintendent Peter Vibart, 'The Terrible Twins', was Scotland Yard's most successful detective. He had very recently convicted the penultimate Great Train Robber and was closing in on the late-Bruce Reynolds, the leader of the robbers, tidying-up his paperwork and preparing for his retirement, due in eleven months' time.

Butler attended the scene, advised Millen and Chitty on the path of the investigation, and agreed to loan some of his Flying Squad officers to the enquiry.

Senior Investigating Officer

Detective Superintendent Richard (Dick) Chitty had been born in Chilworth, a village of 2,000 residents, situated three miles south-east of Guildford in Surrey. The son of a market gardener, he was set to join the family business when, during an argument, his father told him that he did not know what he would do for a living if he did not have the option of joining the family business. Richard immediately retaliated by running off and submitting an application for the Met.

He went to the Metropolitan Police Training School in Westminster in August 1939, a couple of weeks before the UK declared war on Germany. From the Training School, he was posted to Putney Police Station to walk a beat, and from there he went to West End Central as a detective constable for three years, before volunteering for the Royal Air Force and becoming a navigator in a bomber squadron, where he earned the nickname 'Cherty'.

Soon after the war he re-joined the Met and was promoted to Detective Sergeant. Further promotions to Detective Inspector and Detective Chief Inspector, both at Hammersmith, followed in due course. At the time of the incident he was waiting to be promoted to Detective Chief Superintendent and eventually went on to reach the rank of Deputy Assistant Commissioner.

A veteran of 14 previous murder investigations, Chitty had only come back from giving evidence in the latest case the day before the incident at Shepherd's Bush. Returning to find himself in third place in the frame, he was confident that he had time before his next job and planned to spend the forthcoming weekend at his new home in Kent.

At this time, Scotland Yard frequently and regularly provided experienced senior officers to support smaller city and county police forces to investigate murders and serious crimes. Outside the offices of the top men in the CID was a wooden frame, which always had the names of the next three detective superintendents to be sent out at short notice. This lead to detectives excusing themselves from joining colleagues for a drink after work by saying, 'I can't, I'm in the frame,' or the top men at the Yard, on being told of a murder in a county force asking, 'OK, who's in the frame for this one?'

Each detective superintendent had his own 'bag carrier', a detective sergeant (1st class) who would accompany him and support him by managing the Incident Room. The bag was a Gladstone bag and at any time three of these were held, fully stocked with the torches, bags, bottles, pens, paper, tweezers, magnifying glasses, etc. that experience had shown would be required at the scene of a murder. On this occasion, Chitty was assisted by Det Sgt Ted Fosbury.

Metropolitan Police Central Record of Service

Richard Claude CHITTY

Warrant Number:	85/128125
National Insurance:	Not known
Born:	16/12/15 Chilworth, Surrey.
Joined Metropolitan Police:	4/9/39
Height:	5'09"
Marital status:	Married
Education:	Elementary
Former trade or calling:	Shop Assistant
Former police service:	None
Former military service:	RAF 19/9/43–23/8/45 Sgt 1895944
Long service and good conduct medal:	9/2/62

Date	District	Borough	Promoted to
4/9/39	V	Kingston	PC 233
16/6/47	C	Westminster	DC
7/4/55	C6	Fraud Squad	DS2
1/4/58	V	Kingston	DS1
7/7/58	C1	Murder Squad	
23/10/61	N	Islington	DI
4/12/61	V	Kingston	
12/6/62	F	Hammersmith and Fulham	DCI (1/6/64)
3/1/66	C1	Murder Squad	Det Supt
19/11/67	C6	Fraud Squad	DCS
1/10/69	C1	Murder Squad	Commander
1/4/70	DAC C Ops	2 I/C MP CID	DAC
15/12/72	Retired	33 years 103 days	Age 57 (limit)
11/1/83	Died		

Next of kin
Wife and son (born 1944).

Investigating Officer

Detective Chief Inspector John (Ginger) Hensley was second in charge of the CID office at Hammersmith Police Station. At 4.30 pm he was in the CID office at the sub-divisional office at Chiswick when he became the first CID officer to hear about the events at Shepherd's Bush. He immediately called Millen to inform him and was rewarded by being appointed the investigating officer. He promptly summoned Detective Sergeant Begg, who had assisted him on many major enquiries and they both made their way to Braybrook Street.

Metropolitan Police Central Record of Service

John Clifford Austin HEMSLEY

Warrant Number:	61/128495
National Insurance:	Not known
Born:	15/4/20 Barry, Glamorgan
Joined Metropolitan Police:	18/3/46
Height:	5'10.75"
Marital status:	Married
Education:	Secondary
Former trade or calling:	Draughtsmen
Former police service:	None
Former military service:	Army RAC/RAOC 30/11/39–10/5/46
Long service and good conduct medal:	21/6/68

Date	District	Borough	Promoted to
24/6/46	C	Westminster	PC
20/6/49	F	Hammersmith and Fulham	DC
17/4/50	C8	Flying Squad	
30/11/53	F	Hammersmith and Fulham	
20/2/56	C8	Flying Squad	DS2
3/12/60	V	Kingston	
19/7/62	C8	Flying Squad	DI

Date	District	Borough	Promoted to
27/4/64	W	Wandsworth	
4/1/65	C1	Murder Squad	DCI
4/10/65	T	Hounslow	Det Supt
4/5/70	C1	Murder Squad	DCS
31/8/75	Retired	Age 55 (limit)	29 years 167 days
24/9/77	Died		

Next of kin
None recorded

The Forensic Scientist

Detective Superintendent Squires of the Fingerprint Branch went to the scene to take charge of the forensic examination and the collection of exhibits.

The Ace Thief-Taker

Det Insp Jack Slipper was in charge of a team of three of 'London's Finest' detectives, in a Flying Squad Rover saloon, patrolling his old stomping ground in Acton a couple of miles away, when he heard the initial call to Shepherd's Bush and must have arrived within a couple of minutes of the incident.

Slipper was a detective inspector on the Flying Squad at this time. He had joined the Squad on New Year's Day in 1962 as a detective sergeant (2nd class) and been promoted to detective sergeant (1st class) and then detective inspector at the same time as taking a leading role in the investigation of the Great Train Robbery. He would eventually finish up as the detective chief superintendent in charge of the Flying Squad, the job that Tommy Butler currently occupied. Having recently seen the conviction the last of the known train robbers, he was seeking new challenges and was not a man to miss this opportunity.

Metropolitan Police Central Record of Service

John Kenneth Slipper

Warrant Number:	19/136886
National Insurance:	Not known
Born:	20/4/24 Ealing
Joined Metropolitan Police:	30/4/51
Height:	6'3"
Marital status:	Married
Education:	Elementary
Former trade or calling:	Electrician
Former police service:	None
Former military service:	

Date	District	Borough	Promoted to
30/4/51	TS	Training School	PC
13/8/51	T	Richmond	
3/12/51	B	Kensington	
7/5/56	T	Richmond	DC
4/11/57	F	Hammersmith	
8/9/58	T	Richmond	
1/1/62	C8	Flying Squad	DS(2) DS(1) 31/3/64 DI 11/7/66
8/1/67	Q	Harrow	DCI 2/9/68
4/10/71	C10	Stolen Vehicle Squad	DCS
5/3/73	C8	Flying Squad	
4/1/77	Q	Harrow	Uniform CS
24/12/79	Retired	28 years 239 days	Exemplary

Next of kin
Married with two children

Another Detective

Detective Inspector Ronald Steventon was also involved in the investigation. Later, under Sir Robert Mark, Commissioner of Police for the Metropolis between 1972 and 1977, he was appointed to investigate allegations of corruption made against the police and went on to retire with the rank of deputy assistant commissioner.

The Officer in Charge of Q-Cars on F-Division

Kenneth Coote was a slim, quiet spoken, pipe smoker. He was a detective inspector in the CID at Shepherd's Bush and his duties included managing the Q-car and giving the crew a daily briefing. As mentioned in *Chapter 1,* on the day of the shootings, he was at Marylebone Magistrate's Court as officer in the case of a team of five men who had been charged in connection with a prison break at Wormwood Scrubs Prison in June 1965.

The Q-car crew had delivered him to court with all his bulky exhibits, such as grappling ropes for climbing the prison walls, in the morning. At 3 pm Det Insp Coote had arranged for a radio message to be sent to the car asking that they call him back. He had been the last person to speak to Det Sgt Head when Head had called him at the gaoler's office and arranged to pick him up. Foxtrot One-One was on its way to the court to pick up Coote up when they came across the Standard Vanguard.

Metropolitan Police Central Record of Service	
Kenneth John Osmond COOTE	
Warrant Number:	06/128725
National Insurance:	BTA/58/59/04/0
Born:	28/11/23 North Hackney
Joined Metropolitan Police:	3/6/46
Height:	5'09.75'
Marital status:	Married
Education:	Elementary (higher grade)

Former trade or calling:	Clerk	
Former police service:	None	
Former military service:	RN Sub Lieutenant 24/2/42–25/7/46	
Long service and good conduct medal	15/10/68	

Date	District	Borough	Promoted to
2/9/46	C	Westminster	PC 132
8/12/52	T	Hounslow	DC
1/12/56	C1	Murder Squad	DS2
22/10/62	V	Kingston	DS1
3/12/62	B	Kensington and Chelsea	
2/12/63	C11	Criminal Intelligence	
10/1/66	F (FS)	Hammersmith and Fulham	DI
3/6/67	F (FD)	Hammersmith and Fulham	
22/7/68	X	Ealing	
4/1/71	C2	CID Correspondence	
30/4/78	Resigned	31 years 332 days	54 years

Next of kin
Wife (married 15/8/53) and two girls (born 7/8/56 and 11/4/59).

The Inside Team

The nucleus of the inside team, under Det Insp Coote, were Detective Sergeants Robert Berry, Sheila Acton and Ronald Lawrence from the forensic science laboratory, and Detective Constable Clive Martin. The job of the inside team is immensely important and complicated. Every message, no matter how small or apparently insignificant, must be recorded and cross-indexed in those pre-computer days using a by modern standards laborious, relatively ineffective and slow card index system. There were times when this team were handling many hundreds of messages a day taking perhaps hours to do what could nowadays be accomplished in minutes.

Home Office Pathologist

As he left to make his way to Shepherd's Bush, Commander Ernie Millen put a call through to the home of Dr Donald Teare, the Home Office Pathologist to summon the famous scientist to the scene of the crime.

CHAPTER 5

The Investigation

'The Bush', as both policemen and criminals call Shepherd's Bush Police Station, became the heart of the investigation. Minor crimes had to be taken over by junior detectives as often as possible, but the uniformed men still paraded at 6 am, 2 pm and 10 pm for their various tours of duty, for the normal life of a police station had to go on, despite the feverish activity brought about by the murders.

But there was an understandable human difference this time. This time Chris Head was a victim rather than an investigator, and the squad was investigating his murder, and those of his colleagues. This time the officers knew the victims very well, and this time there was a personal touch. Geoffrey Fox, the driver, had walked the beats from that station for many years. More recently, Detective Sergeant Head and Detective Constable Wombwell had arrived there in the CID. And it was from 'the Bush' that they went through the busy streets, and met their deaths.

The Shepherd's Bush Massacre came exceptionally close to being the 'perfect crime'. It was unplanned, spontaneous and motiveless and much of the crime scene, the Standard Vanguard estate, was driven clean away within seconds of the crime being committed. All the witnesses to the crime were young children playing football a few yards away. The first officers on the scene found the Q-car, and the bodies of the three officers, but the suspects had left nothing behind other than their bullets.

The crime scene was subjected to what Ernie Millen, the head of the CID and Det Insp Jack Slipper, later head of the Flying Squad, described as the most vigorous and complete forensic examination that had ever been conducted. Every house in the area was visited; every pedestrian was questioned; a fingertip search was made of the street and the playing fields; all the forensic evidence was collected. Unfortunately, even after all this work there were no further clues. The police officers continued to work through the night, searching the area. All the houses in Braybrook Street left their front doors open all night and a supply of tea and sandwiches for the officers as they searched for clues.

Tracing the Owner of the Standard Vanguard

Chitty and his team got their first clue even before the first police officer arrived at the scene of the incident. Bryan Deacon, a 31-year-old local security guard, drove into Braybrook Street with his wife a few seconds after the murders. Suddenly and without warning he saw a blue Standard Vanguard estate car reverse towards him at a reckless speed, narrowly missing his vehicle.

Fearing that there had been a gaol break from the nearby Wormwood Scrubs Prison, Deacon yelled to his wife to get the number of the car, and made a mental note of it himself. As the Standard Vanguard disappeared into the distance, Deacon drove into nearby Erconwald Street, where he knew that there was a butcher's shop from where he could call the police. As he stopped and got out of his car, Deacon saw a body lying in the road. A few seconds later he saw another body lying underneath the police car in the middle of the road. Deacon called the police via the 999 system and reported the incident. The description of the vehicle was circulated to all cars, but despite all the police cars heading for the scene in the opposite direction to the Standard Vanguard, which was heading away from the scene, no trace was found of it.

Bryan Deacon gave the piece of paper bearing the index number of the Standard Vanguard to PC David Owen who was sitting in the driving seat of an R/T car at the scene. He immediately circulated it. Said Deacon:

'We went back to my parent's house, and I took Pat to work that night for company. When the three detectives came after my phone call, they brought a uniformed man with them to look after the factory. After we made a statement we went to Scotland Yard to look at pictures of criminals, but we couldn't pick any out—the car passed too quickly.

Early next morning we went to Shepherd's Bush to make an addition to our statements. The place was crowded with policemen, coming and going. We saw Mr Chitty for a few seconds in the car park, and he thanked us for coming forward. We hadn't been home long—it was about three o'clock in the morning—when my stomach was suddenly knotted up with terrible pains. I was alright at the time when it happened, but the pain must have been the shock working out. The doctor gave me some medicine, and I was back at work in a couple of days. But I don't ever want to see it again.'

His wife survived the ordeal well, and on 16 October, nine weeks after the shooting, gave birth to an eleven pound baby boy, 13 days late, and without complications.

During their enquiries at the scene, police traced two young children who had been playing football within a hundred yards of the murders. Ten-year-old Jimmy Newton and 14-year-old Tommy McCormack, both of nearby Mellitus Street, were unable to describe the murderers but confirmed that the men had been in the blue estate car which Deacon had seen. Another, unnamed, young witness, who had also been play-ing football nearby, reported that the driver of the Standard Vanguard resembled his footballing hero, Bobby Charlton, a description which fortunately later proved to be extremely accurate when the driver was identified.

The murders were committed on a Friday afternoon at 3.15 pm and by the time that the officers had secured the scene and completed their forensic examination of it, the staff at the Greater London Council Vehi-cle Licensing Centre at County Hall, in Black Prince Road, London, had taken advantage of 'POETS Day' and gone home for the weekend. Fortunately, the Met police had been given their own key to the centre for out-of-hours access. When they visited the registered keeper of the vehicle, he told them that he had recently sold it and notified the centre. Despite their scepticism, the detectives returned to County Hall, where further enquiries revealed that the records were indeed out-of-date and they discovered the name and address of the current keeper.

At 8.30 pm Det Insp Ronald Steventon went to Fernhead Road in Paddington with a police sergeant to see the new registered keeper, John

Edward Witney, a 36-year-old unemployed lorry driver. Witney was at home with his wife in their basement flat but the officers immediately noticed that Witney seemed agitated and that he was trembling and perspiring freely.

When Witney attempted to answer the officers' questions his wife expressed surprise and said, 'What's going on? You never told me!' That was enough for the officers and they asked him to accompany them to Harrow Road Police Station for further questioning. He was later arrested and transferred to Shepherd's Bush where he was locked up. In the early hours of the morning he was interviewed by Det Supt Chitty and a state-ment was taken from him, which took two hours and 20 minutes to take down. In it, Witney continued to deny owning the car but the officers felt pretty confident that they had captured the first of the murderers.

During the investigation, Witney put forward a really unlikely alibi. He insisted over and over again that he had sold the Vanguard the pre-vious day, the day of the murders, at lunchtime. He had been, he said, in a pub called the *Clay Pigeon* in Eastcote. In the car park, he had met a man who wanted to buy an old banger and after a bit of bargaining he'd sold it for a 'score', £20, a tenner down, and he'd get the rest when he handed over the logbook at a meeting arranged for the following day. Witney said that, after the sale, he had taken a bus home and killed some time at Shepherd's Bush Green and in a betting shop in Acton Vale; he had not wanted to go home too early as his wife did not know that he was out of work.

No one believed the story, especially as by then the footballing boy had told the police that one of the men in the Vanguard looked like Bobby Charlton—a description which could well have applied to Witney. But disbelieving is not enough. A lie has to be disproved and, what is harder still, the evidence to break an alibi has to be sufficiently substantial to stand up in court, perhaps months later, when the case comes to trial.

Detective Inspector Jack Slipper was given the job of breaking this alibi, but he had no reason to know just how tricky that would be. For a detective who really knows his patch, it can be a very small world. Slipper knew of Witney already, but what was more important, he personally knew the manager of the betting shop who could make or break the story.

Because they knew each other, Slipper planned the approach to the manager carefully. He knew that barging in with a heavy-handed formal approach would be a mistake. The betting shop manager—we'll call him Sammy Henderson—wasn't a villain, but he was a useful sort of chap, a very experienced and quick-thinking man, who knew his way around and, who was, unfortunately, very close to Witney's family, which meant a lot in a closely-knit community like Acton.

Slipper went to the betting shop at five-thirty on Saturday afternoon and caught Henderson just when he knew the shop would be closing. He took him to a pub across the road and found a quiet corner; then over a pint he laid out the problem. When you want a written statement from a man like Henderson, the last thing you do is mention it. The line Slipper took was that Sammy was the man in the middle and he was someone who might be able to save him some embarrassment.

Henderson knew from Slipper's earlier Acton days how he'd handled other cases, for example the housewives' electrical fraud, so he could look him in the eye when he explained to him what a dreadful situation the alibi had put him in. Sammy believed Slipper when he said that he would try and save him embarrassment with Witney's family if he could. Sammy's attitude was that Witney was just a mug who could not possibly have been involved in a triple police murder.

Slipper made it clear that there was no doubt that Witney was involved, and that Sammy should not waste the chance that he was offering him to have him, Slipper, as an ally, not an enemy. Again, Henderson knew from the old days that it was not an empty offer, but he also knew that while Slipper always tried to be fair, he was also very determined: Slipper was not going to be put off, whatever happened, so he might as well come clean with him.

Gradually, over a second pint, Slipper got Henderson's confidence and teased the truth out of him. Witney had not been near the betting shop. Henderson had every reason to be sure of that, even though he worked in a back room. He told Slipper that Witney often came to the shop, but that he was always 'on the earhole'—out to borrow money. Henderson was sick of him, and if Witney had come in the man at the front of the shop who marked the boards would have immediately warned him.

When Slipper was satisfied that Henderson had told him everything, it was time to get to the awkward bit. Slipper was glad that Henderson was sensible enough to tell him the truth, he said, but he needed it all in writing. But because Slipper knew Henderson's character and the circles he moved in, he still did not take a fully official line with him. 'It's got to be put in writing, Sammy,' he said, 'there's no way around it. All we have to work out is how best to do it without making you look too bad with Witney's family'.

'There's no way I can do it,' Sammy said, 'not without talking to a few people first. You know that'. Slipper did know that, but it did not make his own chance any easier. To play it by the book, he should not have let Sammy out of his sight until he had made a formal statement. If he refused to make it there and then Slipper should have taken him back to the police station and insisted that he write down everything he had just told him.

But Slipper knew that Sammy could still wriggle out. He wasn't stupid enough to pretend that he'd seen Witney, lying to support an alibi involving a triple police murder was not in his character. But Slipper wanted more than that. He wanted it in writing that Henderson would have been told if Witney had entered the betting shop. Henderson was under no legal obligation to do that. If Slipper put him under pressure in a police station he could have squirmed out of it and said, 'Well I didn't see him. But I was in my office all afternoon. I can't be sure of everything that happens in the shop itself…' So Slipper decided to gamble. 'All right Sammy,' he said, 'I'll come back tomorrow morning. I'll give you tonight to see the people you have to talk to'.

Slipper was sure he'd made the right decision, but when he got back to the station and told Dick Chitty and Tommy Butler what he'd done, they nearly gave birth on the spot! They simply could not believe he'd been so unorthodox, with three colleagues dead. Slipper held his ground, but he knew Chitty did not need telling when he said, 'I'm sure I'm right, guv'nor, but if we don't get the statement, I know it will be down to me'.

The next morning, Sunday, Slipper went to Sammy Henderson's house at eight o'clock with Sergeant George Garbut and sat with Henderson and his wife during a tense and gloomy breakfast. The two men had the measure of each other so well that Slipper did not have to produce any more arguments to convince Sammy. All he said was, 'Sammy, you know it doesn't give me any pleasure to ask you to give me evidence that will put someone close to you away for life. But I'm sure you couldn't live with yourself if you lied to save him. You know that as well as I do. This isn't like covering up for someone who's been buying and selling a bit of gear'. 'I know it,' Sammy answered, 'I've talked to a couple of people and I know I've got to do it. I'll give you your statement'.

The statement broke the alibi completely. Sammy did not try to hedge. He told Slipper he had not seen Witney at the betting shop and that he was certain he would have been told if he had shown his face there. Later that morning, Slipper took a statement from the man who had been working on the counter at the betting shop, confirming what Sammy had said. When Slipper handed the two statements to Chitty, they both knew that he'd been right to gamble, but the look in Chitty's eyes told him that it was just as well that he had won.

Tracing the Vehicle

Appeals for information about the blue Standard Vanguard estate PGT 726 had been broadcast on TV and radio, and reports of possible sightings were pouring in. On Saturday night, just over 24 hours after the murders, it was traced by an observant member of the public who had seen it being driven up Tinworth Street in Lambeth. At this time this was a narrow cul-de-sac leading only to the railway arches under the tracks approaching Waterloo Station. Ironically, today Tinworth Street houses the headquarters of the National Crime Agency, the unit taking the lead in tackling organized crime. The speed at which it was being driven, and the fact that the driver had scratched the car along a wall, had given the man the feeling that there was something wrong.

The man who had found the vehicle called the police and reported what he had seen and officers immediately went to the scene. In a garage under a railway arch they saw, by the light of a torch, a blue estate car. The garage door was forced open and then they saw the entire vehicle, index number PGT 726. Fingerprint officers and photographers busied themselves with the car. The fingerprints were photographed and rushed to the Criminal Records Office for possible identification. Meanwhile, other officers found a pair of car number plates in the back of the car, essential kit for car thieves; part of a nylon stocking which could be used as a mask; and most important of all, three .38 cartridges, all recently fired. Like the Q-car earlier, this car was towed to Theobalds Road. There it was put in what one might call 'forensic quarantine': locked in a special steel cage where it could be preserved for detailed examination in exactly the state in which it had been found.

The Standard Vanguard estate getaway vehicle discovered by the police in Lambeth, south-London before
the killers were able to remove and dispose of it.

The three cartridges were examined by the ballistics expert, John McCafferty, who was able to establish that they had been fired from the same gun. Enquiries revealed that the garage in which the car had been found had been rented in Witney's name. Fingerprint experts found that the fingerprints in the car belonged to Witney.

Proving Witney Parked the Vanguard in the Garage

When the police had the Standard Vanguard estate in their possession and were able to show that Witney was the registered keeper, they had a good case against him; but it would be a much stronger case if they were able to prove that it was also Witney who had recently parked the car in the garage. This would prove that he had been lying when he said that he had sold the car the day before in Eastcote in Middlesex; and raise questions about what had been his motive for lying. The answer to which was that perhaps that he had been concerned in murdering three police officers. Again Jack Slipper was tasked with interviewing the garage owner and investigating whether he was able to supply such a statement.

It would not matter if he had not seen Witney after the crime because it would have been too much of a coincidence for any jury to accept that a man had bought a car casually in a public house in Eastcote in Middlesex and then garaged it at exactly the place in Kennington that the registered owner had used, across the other side of London.

Slipper arranged to meet the garage owner at his flat in Victoria and take him to Shepherd's Bush for an identity parade. On the way the owner assured Slipper that he *would* be able to identify the Vanguard's owner, but Slipper was not convinced. His witness was too nervous. His hands were sweating and his brow was damp. Inwardly he was shaking and there is nothing worse at an identity parade. When a witness is scared, he does not look properly at the faces in the line and just wanders up and down in a daze. When they arrived, Slipper was pleased to hear that in his absence, Witney had asked for a confrontation instead of an identity parade. Now, the garage owner only had to look at Witney and say 'yes' or 'no'. Slipper felt that in these circumstances they might still be alright.

Witney was brought into the charge room, where he was confronted by the garage owner. The two men clearly exchanged looks and Slipper felt sure that he had the right man, but the garage owner would not make the identification. He looked Witney up and down a couple of times and said nervously, 'No. It is not him. But it is so much like him, it is unbelievable'. It was a bombshell. The detectives all felt gutted. They were sure that they had the right man but the garage owner's refusal to identify Witney would only encourage him in his ridiculous alibi. The police still had good evidence, but it was circumstantial, and if they were going to have any chance of catching the rest of the team they had to break Witney down quickly. Dick Chitty arranged to call his troops together for a briefing later that evening and Slipper was ordered to go upstairs with the garage owner and take a written statement, detailing the outcome of the confrontation with Witney.

The situation was extremely delicate. Slipper felt sure the man was lying, but as a police officer taking a statement, he was under a legal obligation not to influence the wording. If he tried to suggest what the man should say, the statement could be challenged in court, even if it turned out to be the truth.

Nowadays, a witness is obliged to sign an endorsement to a statement which warns him that he can be prosecuted if he knowingly states something that it untrue. At that time, Slipper did not have the benefit of such an endorsement, but he made it clear to the man that with the murder of three policemen involved the investigation would be so thorough that it was very much in his interests to be completely truthful. So please would he be very careful not to state anything he would not be willing to repeat in the witness box at what would probably be the trial of the decade. At first the man did not react, then, suddenly, he looked up from the paper and said, 'Officer, I'd like to complete this statement later. I'd like to discuss it first with my wife and family'.

Slipper knew then that he was getting somewhere and he took the garage owner quickly back to his flat in Victoria. He asked for two hours alone. Slipper left him and shot across London to do another, quite separate task, then went back to the flat at about nine o'clock. When he got there, he found an extraordinary scene. What looked like his whole family was gathered around—his wife, his children, some aunts and uncles, even a cousin or two, and the atmosphere was like a wake.

When Slipper went in, the garage owner took him aside and solemnly said, 'I'd like to come back with you now and make a fresh statement. I wasn't telling the truth. Witney was the man, without any doubt'. Slipper explained to him that he did not want a fresh statement; he should just complete the statement he had already begun, explaining his change of mind after the two hour break. Slipper put in a quick call to the Bush and gave them the news in time to change the whole atmosphere of Chitty's briefing. It turned out later that the garage owner had held back not because of fear of reprisals from Witney, but because Witney and the two other killers had been stealing metal from a firm over in Acton, and the garage owner had been taking loads off them and was afraid of being charged with receiving.

Charging Witney

The detectives were now satisfied that Witney was one of the murderers. Chitty called his team together and then decided to charge him that 'with others' he had murdered the three policemen in Braybrook Street. The charges were read to Witney and he was taken back to his cell.

Soon after he was returned to his cell, around midnight, Witney asked to see Detective Chief Inspector 'Ginger' Hensley in his cell. With his alibi shattered and his car located, he 'put his hands up' and confessed. He knew that he did have not a chance. He said, 'As God is my judge, I had nothing to do with the shooting of the three policemen. I just drove into Braybrook Street where a small car pulled up alongside. Two men got out and one asked if it was my car. I said, "Yes". Then he asked me for my road fund licence and I told him I hadn't got one. The elder of the two policemen walked around to the other side of the car and said, "Let's have a look in here." Without anything further, Roberts leant across and shot the young officer in the face. The sound of the shot deafened and dazed me. The other officer ran to the front, and Roberts, followed by Duddy, gave chase, still shooting. I saw the second officer stumble and fall. Roberts fired again, I don't know how many times. Duddy raced alongside and shot through the window of the police car. They ran back to the car, jumped in and said, "Drive!"'

The detectives were doing well! Less than 36 hours after the crime they were one up and two to go. They now knew the names of the other two suspects. Criminal record checks revealed that they had both been in trouble with the police, and that Roberts had convictions for violence.

Catching Duddy

Unfortunately, although Witney had named his two associates to the police, he did not know their addresses; but he did know the way to the places where they lived, having picked them up in his car to take them out 'to work' in recent weeks. So that night, lying in the back of the police car and covered with a blanket, he was smuggled out of Shepherd's Bush Police Station. He went with Jack Slipper to Wymering Road, Maida Vale, where he pointed out Roberts' flat, and then to another block of flats off Ladbroke Grove, where he said that Duddy lived.

While Witney was taken back to his cell, both flats were cordoned off, and police with dogs and an officer with a tear gas gun at the ready, moved in. But there was no sign of Roberts at the first address, and at the second address the police found only Duddy's scared teenage daughters. The girls said they had not seen their father in the last week.

Then came surprising news from Fleet Street. The *Daily Mirror* newsroom had received a call from a man who claimed he was John Duddy. He rang once early in the morning, before the staff had arrived, and then again just before eleven o'clock and spoke to reporter Edward Vale. The conversation, which was recorded on a dictaphone, seemed genuine enough. The voice was slightly Scottish, and the author sounded as though he was in trouble, and he said he wanted legal advice, claiming that he had no part in the shooting. The transcript was as follows:

Duddy: 'This is Duddy. If I didn't do the shooting do I get done just the same as the others?'

Vale: 'Well, we've got a ... we have a lawyer. The Daily Mirror senior lawyer here'.

Duddy: 'I haven't got to talk to him — look, I'll tell you what. You offer to meet me ... now I'll tell you. I'll meet you. Listen'.

Vale: 'Okay. Where do you suggest?'

Duddy: 'A smell of a copper ... if there's a smell of a copper I'll be off'.

Vale: 'There'll be no sign of a copper at all'.

Duddy: 'Right now, I'll meet you on Turnham Green'.

Vale: 'Turnham Green?'

Duddy: 'Yes, there's a cricket pitch on Turnham Green'.

Vale: 'Yes'.

Duddy: '…and I will meet you there at half past 12. Now, I'm telling you, the smell of a copper — I'm away'.

Vale: 'That's fair enough, okay. What time do you suggest?'

Duddy: 'At half past 12'.

Vale: 'Okay, now look. I'm about six feet tall, I'm wearing a navy blue suit with a spotted tie and carrying a copy of today's Daily Mirror marked "voucher"'.

Duddy: 'It'll be you then?'

Vale: 'Yes. I'll be carrying under my arm a copy of today's Daily Mirror with the word "voucher" on it'.

Duddy: 'I'll meet you at half past 12'.

Vale: 'At half past 12'.

Duddy: 'I canna afford to hang on. If there's a smell of a copper I'll be away'.

Vale: 'I understand that. Now, do you want me to bring a lawyer with me?'

Duddy: 'No, I want to speak…I just want to speak to one man'.

Vale: 'Twelve-thirty at Turnham Green. I'll be there myself'.

There was then a pause and he was gone.

A representative of the *Daily Mirror* telephoned Supt Chitty at Shepherd's Bush to tell him of the arrangements, and then five reporters drove to Turnham Green. Vale went separately in a chauffeur driven car, so that he could at least appear to be alone. It was a nightmare drive from Fleet Street through west London. The warm, sunny weather seemed to have brought out every car in the city and there were traffic jams all the way. In one place the reporters were blocked by a furniture pantechnicon, and the slightly deaf driver would move only after the reporters had bawled the explanation of their haste into his car. Even so, they made the cricket field in time and Vale strode to the pitch and sat down, a copy of the *Daily Mirror* in plain sight.

It was still a few minutes to half past 12 as the reporters moved to inconspicuous observation points around the field. By now the sun was blazing hot, attracting many local workers to spend their lunch-hour at leisure on the grass, and in amongst them were detectives, sprawled but watchful on the man in the middle. At the end of the field, sitting in shirtsleeves, his collar open, was Det Ch Insp Hensley, with a pretty policewoman in a summer frock. Several of the other men apparently relaxing on the grass were policemen and some of the girls in summer frocks were policewomen.

A dozen photographers had moved quietly into as many houses which had overlooking windows, and every camera was trained on Edward Vale. If Duddy had arrived, there is no doubt he would have been collected, and that the scene would have been well recorded on film. But the minutes ticked by into an hour and at the end of two hours the ambush was called off. Was it an ordinary hoax, or had Duddy arrived and spotted the police or the press? It took us but half an hour to find the truth.

In a local public house where the reporters went for a glass of beer, the radio was on and a crowd of enthusiastic punters was listening to an exciting race when the cool voice of an announcer came through and said, 'We must interrupt the racing to give you an important news announcement. John Duddy, whom police wish to interview in connection with the murder of three policemen in Braybrook Street, Hammersmith, has been arrested in Glasgow'.

Chitty had heard the news by telephone from Det Ch Insp Bob Brown, of the Glasgow CID. He had been in touch with Shepherd's Bush before because he knew the Duddy family and, in particular, Duddy's brother, Vincent. Inspector Brown had already made several raids in Glasgow, and on that day he had a positive tip. With two other armed detectives and Vincent Duddy he went to a tenement in Stephenson Street, Calton, a crumbling housing estate, and crept silently up the rickety stairs to the third floor. Brother Vincent said, 'It's me, Vinny'. Then the police burst in to find Duddy lying on his bed, he seemed to be numbed. He was taken to a waiting police car, which was surrounded by other detectives, put on the floor, his head covered with a blazer, and driven to police headquarters.

Back in London, Supt Chitty instructed Ch Insp Hensley and Insp Jack Slipper to fly to Glasgow. At the same time, he put out a radio call to his team of detectives who had been concentrating in the Notting Hill area of west London where Duddy was known to frequent a number of clubs. After several days working long hours, and with two of the suspects in custody, he decided to reward his officers by arranging for them to have a drink in the *Beaumont Arms*. After a couple of hours the party was disrupted when the publican shouted, 'Thief, thief!' A burglar in the private part of the pub was surprised to find himself being confronted by 50 of London's finest detectives. In the incident room at The Bush flights were selected, tickets purchased and arrangements made.

Later that night Duddy was driven from Glasgow CID headquarters to Glasgow Airport at Abbotsinch, where a huge crowd had collected. He sat in the back seat of the first car, between the two Scotland Yard men. They were followed by another black car carrying Det Ch Supt Tom Goodall, the chief of the Glasgow CID.

The police cars sped through the city streets and when they got into open country reached speeds of over 70 miles per hour on the ten mile trip to the airport. Hundreds of people looked out of the windows of the terminal building as the cars drove onto the tarmac and stopped at the bottom of the aircraft gangway. Duddy was handcuffed and, with a coat over his head, hustled up the gangway steps to where 22-year-old stewardess Miss Patricia Docherty was waiting. She showed them into seats in the rear portion of the plane, which was completely cut off from the forward section. Duddy and the two detectives sat in a row on the port side, where the windows were curtained. On the journey, Miss Docherty served the party refreshments and over the loudspeaker system Captain Harry Lea described the journey over the Solway Firth and the Lake District, which must have seemed ironical to Duddy, knowing, as he must have, that his chances of freedom during the rest of his life, were slim.

A lazy, incompetent, inexperienced police officer who had seen the reports of the massacre of the police officers in Shepherd's Bush, then been involved in the enquiry into the incident, and then been asked to collect one of the men responsible, may have felt that he had a 'duty' to beat the suspect up and possibly put his life at risk. Most readers would be amazed that any police officer could feel this way, but I can assure them that some can. Professional and skilled investigators like Hensley and Slipper knew that they had a job to do, to bring Duddy back safely, going to any lengths to protect him from danger. They needed him to stand trial, in order to protect the reputation of the British police, the MPS and the Flying Squad, as well as their own reputations.

Hensley and Slipper were two of Scotland Yard's very best detectives, experienced in some of the most serious crimes in the previous twenty years. They treated Duddy as a long-lost brother. They spoke to him as an equal, discussing the crime as a simple matter of fact, without displaying their emotions, or judging him. They secured his confidence and hoped that *just maybe* he would confess his sins to them. That is what happened. Duddy had expected a beating, and was surprised, and no doubt relieved, when Hensley and Slipper considerately gave him a coat to put over his head so that he did not have to face the press and the crowds that would be waiting along the route for a glimpse of the 'cop killer'.

In the plane, Duddy complained of feeling uncomfortable, so Slipper let him slide down under the seats and take the covering off. He also let him have a cigarette, brought him a coffee, and generally tried to make him comfortable. It was the last thing Duddy expected and the officers' attitude really shook him. Suddenly, he turned to Slipper and said, 'Look, I've got to tell you. It was me who shot the driver. Roberts yelled out, "Get the gun and shoot". And I got out of the Vanguard and ran up to the police car and shot the driver through the head. I must have been mad. I wish you could hang me now'.

Slipper cautioned Duddy, got Hensley to witness it, and then took down his statement. Later, at the Old Bailey, Duddy's counsel challenged the statement because of a picture taken during the flight which showed Duddy with his head covered. The picture showed the air hostess changing her shoes. The defence counsel suggested that she was changing her shoes at the end of the flight as she prepared to get off the plane, and the fact that Duddy's head was still covered suggested that it must have been covered throughout the flight and that consequently he could not have had a conversation with the officers. Hopefully, the jury would give more weight to who shot who, rather than who was wearing what days after the shooting.

The trip to collect Duddy was covered across the media and appeared on the front page of all the national newspapers. Nobody who saw this could have believed that just eight years later a very similar trip would almost wreck Slipper's career when, in 1974, as detective chief superintendent in charge of the Flying Squad he took Det Insp Peter Jones to Rio de Janeiro in Brazil to collect Ronnie Biggs, a fugitive from the Great Train Robbery.

The police tails were up; three days after the shooting it was two men charged and one to go. But catching the third man, Harry Roberts was not going to be easy and finished up taking three months.

The Search for Harry Roberts

Chitty received useful information about Roberts' whereabouts from a woman Roberts had been with the weekend after the shootings. She told the police that when he left her he had been planning to buy a haversack, a primus stove, and a sleeping bag. This tied in with what he already knew about Roberts' interest in camping and his experience as a soldier in Malaya, where he had training and experience in survival skills and camouflage.

Front page of the *Daily Mirror* indicative of the mass coverage by the media of what remains the biggest and most intense manhunt in British criminal history. This continued with the media playing a highly active role right up to the day when Harry Roberts was caught.

Chitty came to the conclusion that Roberts must be hiding, commando style, in Epping Forest, where he had roamed as a child and camped as a youth. Chitty decided to search the whole of the forest's 6,000 thickly-wooded acres. At dawn on 18 August more than 500 detectives and uniformed men, including dog handlers and the now-famous mobile Commando Squad, the forerunner of the Special Patrol Group and the Territorial Support Group, began a systematic 48-hour yard-by-yard search. Many of the police were armed; others carried staves. They moved ahead like beaters in a shoot, each section linked by short-wave radio to a mobile headquarters.

Every glade was combed, every shed and hut and farmhouse inspected. Nowhere was there any trace of Roberts, and after two days of hunting, the police had to accept the fact that if he had ever been in Epping Forest he had now gone further afield.

Chitty did not entirely forget Epping Forest. He focussed his detectives on the preparation of the case for court, on continuing enquiries into tracing Roberts, and into identifying the source of the weapons used to shoot the police officers.

Roberts' Women

Following the debriefing of the two men in custody who Roberts had been working with in the months leading up to the shootings, Chitty decided his best chance of tracing Roberts came from the women in his life: his mother, his ex-wife and his girlfriends.

Roberts' mother, Dorothy, lived on an estate near Euston. Chitty tasked Slipper with searching her flat and interviewing her about what she knew of her son's life, friends and current whereabouts. She served her visitors tea in china cups and talked sentimentally about her son, who she called 'Robin' and who had vowed to her again-and-again, after every transgression, that he would go straight. Slipper was tasked with keeping surveillance on her and put in charge of a squad of 12 women police constables (WPCs) from police stations and squads across London. Some of the WPCs were detectives, but most were uniformed constables and the idea of working in plain clothes on such an important murder case was just the kind of excitement they had dreamed of. But they soon found out that there is little glamour in surveillance. They spent days upon days sitting in vans outside Roberts' mother's flat, logging the same routine every day—from home to the pub, from the pub to the shops, from the shops back home. The observation had to be kept up.

The police knew by then that Roberts was the only really professional criminal of the three. He did not have much of a record as a crook but he was a dangerous individual. He had served with distinction in the Army in the Far East and had been decorated once as a sniper after sitting unobserved in a tree for 48 hours. Witney claimed that Roberts had shot two of the officers.

His mother was a character, a shrewd old lady who doted on him. Slipper once had to take her to a TV studio, where she recorded an appeal for Roberts to give himself up, but the officers did not believe that she meant a word of it.

Roberts' wife, Margaret, had not seen him for eight years, not since the night when he had beaten her up in a Soho nightclub for refusing to earn money as a prostitute and she had gone to the police and informed them of a robbery with violence that he had committed. For the last six years she had been working in the Midlands and the north of England as a striptease dancer under the name of Mitzi. Because it was known that Roberts had a grudge against her for informing on him and might now attempt to silence her forever she was put under police protection.

Margaret was obviously keenly aware of the threat that Roberts posed to her and very keen to help the police to lock him up in any way that she could. She spent a lot of time with Slipper and a woman detective inspector, checking on the stories that she had told about Roberts' supposed departure from London.

Margaret was a very odd sort of woman to be the lover of a man like Roberts. She was a plain suburban housewife who had left a husband and a couple of kids back in Bristol. She did not talk or live flashily and although she seemed to have no wish to protect Roberts now that it was known that he was a police killer, Slipper was convinced that the stories that she was telling them were part of a false trail laid by Roberts. He was wrong, but at the time he found it frustrating to have to go through her story, step-by-step, when he did not think it was going to lead anywhere.

The story she told was that, after the murders, Roberts had bought camping equipment and clothes for living out of doors. She said that she had accompanied him to the outskirts of London and said goodbye as he, apparently, headed off into the wilds. Slipper did not think that she was necessarily a party to the deception but he did not really believe that Roberts had gone to live in the open. However, the police could not really ignore the lead, and he visited the camping equipment store in Tottenham Court Road and took details of the equipment that Roberts had bought so that it could be circulated to rural police forces. He went over the story again and again, with the girlfriend and the woman detective inspector; they even rode the Green Line bus out to the point where she claimed to have said goodbye to Roberts. Despite all the work, neither wife nor mother could give any clue as to Roberts' possible whereabouts.

The other two important women in Roberts' life were his two landladies June Howard and Lillian Perry. We will hear more about them in *Chapter 8*.

The Arrest of Harry Roberts

Eventually, three months after the incident in Braybrook Street, a 21-year-old farm labourer, John Cunningham, described as a gypsy, went out poaching at night with a catapult in Thorley Wood near Bishops Stortford in Hertfordshire. He saw a light gleaming in the undergrowth and crawled silently towards it until he saw that the glint of light came from a gap in a camouflaged tent. He ran back to his family's caravan and told his father.

Cunningham's father thought little of the incident, until a couple of days later a policeman from Essex Constabulary came to his caravan to make enquiries about a number of thefts recently committed in Bishops Stortford. They told him about the tent in the forest.

As dawn broke the next morning, the police and other officers went into the forest to search for the tent. It was so well camouflaged that, although the gipsies (as they were described) had told them where it was, it was still difficult to find. It was strategically sited so that its inhabitant had an uninterrupted view of anyone approaching. It was excellently constructed, with a framework of boughs and twigs covered by a tarpaulin and camouflaged, in infantry style, with green and brown paint. There was no sign of any occupant.

Roberts' hideaway in Thorley Wood, Hertfordshire expertly constructed using camouflage and survival skills gained in the British Army (see later in the chapter).

Chitty was informed and went to the scene. What he saw left him in no doubt that they had found Roberts' lair. He called on the MPS, Hertfordshire Constabulary and Essex Police for all the police officers that they could spare. He threw a cordon around the area and, confident that Roberts would not move in daylight, he settled down to wait for darkness. They stayed through the night, but in the morning, when it seemed that the owner of the tent would not return, forensic scientists removed articles, including a whisky bottle and gun holster on which were fingerprints. These proved that the occupant of the tent was Roberts.

It was 15 November 1966, just three months, or 96 days, after the shootings, when the police moved in to arrest Roberts, confident that he was secure within their cordon. One police officer has a very special reason for remembering that cold wintry morning over 50 years ago. 33-year-old Stevenage traffic policeman Sgt Peter Smith arrested Roberts. He told the press:

'This morning at six o'clock I left Stevenage with PC John Allen, of Datchworth. We went searching Mathams Wood, and I was on the outside of the wood, about 500 yards from it, as part of an armed police cordon. I was standing by an old disused hangar filled with bales of straw. I took out my revolver for my own safety. Nobody was with me. I began to search the hangar and as I walked through the bales of straw I noticed a bottle of methylated spirits.

The time was 11.50 am. I pulled a bale of straw down and then saw a little Primus stove, a torch and a Luger gun or pistol, and a few other odds and ends. Obviously someone was either sleeping there or had been sleeping there. I pulled another bale away—and below it was Roberts. He was inside his sleeping bag. He made no response at all. As far as I was concerned he was just a sleeping bag, lying in the straw'.

Sergeant Smith poked Roberts with his rifle, and his head, complete with a gingery beard, stuck out. The first words he uttered were, 'Please don't shoot'. Ironically these could so easily have been the same words that his own victims had uttered as he cold-bloodedly gunned them down. On this occasion, as so often in the past, a police officer tendered him the mercy that he had so easily deprived his own victims of.

Smith born in 1933 and later living in North Hertfordshire then related how he had taken Roberts out of the disused hangar near Sawbridgeworth and handed him over to the detectives who would gather and collate the evidence necessary to convict him. After he had completed his notes and related the story to his colleagues, Sgt Smith went home to a nice steak supper, prepared by his wife as a reward for catching Roberts.

Sergeant Peter Smith, left, and Sergeant Oswald Thorne
(who was also involved in the arrest process)

The news that Roberts had, eventually, been arrested in the woods in Hertfordshire, came as some consolation to all the officers who had spent so many days, weeks and months from August through to November searching for him there. Chitty sat opposite him to tell him that he would be charged with three murders; and then waited in silence. Chitty realised that Roberts was likely to clam up if he thought that it would upset the police, because it would make him feel powerful. He also realised that he had been living alone in the woods for 90 days and would be desperate to tell somebody, anybody, his story. Chitty did not ask him any questions; he showed that he didn't care. After a while, Roberts could not hold his silence any longer: he bragged, he showed off, he admitted all his crimes, and told Chitty everything.

Roberts' Life in the Woods

Roberts had installed himself in a trackless corner of Thorley Wood, some six miles from Epping Forest. Having found a patch of thick undergrowth, he had crawled into it, dug a shallow hole, and pitched his tent over it. Next he made a kind of breastwork with the excavated soil, carpeted the earth floor with plastic bags, and camouflaged his tent with more plastic bags painted green and brown. Then he wove a screen of light branches over the whole, installed his sleeping bag, the primus stove, a lamp and two radios, set up an elaborate warning system of trip wires, and dug drains so that his tent would remain watertight even when it rained.

He had, of course, been obliged to steal both the paint and the radios, and he was regularly obliged to steal money (either by breaking into a house or vandalising the coin box of a public telephone) for the purpose of buying food. Every day he listened to *BBC News* items about himself, and most days he bought and read a newspaper. He had kept his camp and cooking utensils spotlessly clean, and he was growing a beard. He was comfortable enough in the warm summer weather and had not so far been disturbed, even though there was a gipsy caravan a few hundred yards away in another part of the wood. Realising that he must steal cash to survive, he returned to the spot on Hampstead Heath where he and Duddy had buried the three guns. Disinterring two of them, he left behind the pistol with which Duddy had murdered Fox, and returned to Thorley Wood.

Then, from local stores, he bought supplies: leather, with which he made a holster for his Luger (he in fact made himself two holsters: one was too big, so that the gun kept falling out; the second was too small and he couldn't get the gun out of it), and cans of food. He paid for them with handfuls of small coins stolen from the telephone box. Politeness prevented most of those who sold him his purchases from commenting on such unusual legal tender.

A reluctance to look foolish in front of friends caused at least one suspicious villager to hold her tongue. 'Gosh, he looked like Harry Roberts,' said a lady in the general store after his first visit. But when her assistant and a customer laughed at her, she felt that she must be wrong and never mentioned it again. Day succeeded day, and Roberts' hideout, never easily detectable, merged more and more into the surrounding undergrowth. The raw earth of his breastwork mellowed, broken branches healed, and trampled grass sprang up anew. After two weeks in the open his face had lost much of its puffiness, his complexion had freshened, his confidence in himself was growing, and Britain's most persistent policemen had resigned themselves to a prolonged search.

They were not in the least discouraged, however. Even though Shepherd's Bush Police Station had received 3,714 phone calls and 521 letters in the 14 days since the triple murder, and dealt with 1,200 sightings of Roberts in the ten days since issuing his description, there was no sense of defeat or futility in Chitty's operations room. Nor was there any feeling that the enquiry had lost its momentum after so early and promising a breakthrough. Policemen are more accustomed, in fact, to wars of attrition, than to swift campaigns of annihilation. Detectives rely not on flashes of brilliant intuition but on the patient, jigsaw assembly of a hundred unspectacular facts into an invincible case against the accused. And Chitty's case against Witney, Duddy and Roberts was already well-nigh invincible, lacking only the killers' guns and Roberts.

Even had Chitty's team begun to weary, continued public interest would have sustained them. Flowers were still being delivered to the station. A card of sympathy had arrived 'From the housewives of Braybrook Street'. Donations to the fund for dependants had topped £157,000. And as a kind of inverted compliment to the indefatigable Flying Squad, London's crime rate had decreased dramatically.

October came and the nights grew colder. Not only that, but soon the leaves would start falling. If Roberts was living rough, the police reasoned, the likelihood of his being discovered would grow by the day as trees and undergrowth shed their lush summer foliage, and damp wood smoked on every outdoor fire.

It was his character, however, not the season that was beginning to imperil Roberts. Having concealed himself in Thorley Wood with a degree of skill and cunning for which his Army instructors would have awarded him the highest marks, he had begun, after six weeks, to behave carelessly. Compelled to forage each night he had begun to raid houses too close to Thorley Wood for his own security; and deprived of human company, which he minded a great deal less than most, he had begun to read at night by lamplight. Both habits were cardinal sins for a fugitive in hostile territory. The first had, sooner or later, to draw the attention of the local police; the second could at any time betray him to any of Thorley Wood's occasional nocturnal prowlers.

Ever self-indulgent, Roberts persistently broke the rules of the game he was playing. Yet reading the newspapers he bought each day by the light of his reckless lamp, or listening to one or other of the two stolen, and potentially treacherous, transistor radios he kept inside his sleeping bag, he must frequently have felt immune to detection, even though he wore, on his daily visits to the store, the most highly publicised face and combat jacket in Britain.

Snug inside his tent in Thorley Wood on October 10, he read that police frogmen were searching a reservoir in distant Cheltenham, because someone had found a rucksack in the area. They searched it for three days. The next day he read that Chitty and his sergeant had flown to Dublin a second time. There the Irish Police had collaborated with Chitty and, by scouring the city and every possible hideout and haunt within a 30 mile radius, had thrown the Republic of Ireland's underworld into a state of vociferous uproar. But they had found no English murderer.

On October 12 he read of the escape from Wormwood Scrubs of his one-time tutor in French, the spy George Blake. Though the headlines left him in no doubt that Britain regarded this as an outrage (Blake had been sentenced to a record 42 years' imprisonment, of which he had served only five-and-a-half), it never occurred to him that there would be renewed speculation in Scotland Yard as to whether he, Harry Roberts, had not, after all, on August 12, been casing The Scrubs with a view to springing George Blake some ten weeks later.

Chitty left the problem of the Blake escape to Insp Coote—who had also to deal with the discovery of a racket in wood alcohol inside the prison from which the escape had been made. Chitty let it be known that he now believed Roberts to be hiding in England, not in Ireland, and as an armed murderer, not a Russian Pimpernel.

In Thorley Wood it was late afternoon and raining, as the murderer lay in his tent, reading. The sound of raindrops falling on his tent was agreeable and reassuring. Indifferent to the rain, three boys scouted through the wood, eyes alert, hunting for rabbits. 'Hey,' said one suddenly, pointing to Roberts' hideout. 'Look at that'. Curious, because no one but the Cunningham family lived in the wood (and they lived in caravans some distance away), the three boys crept up on the elaborately concealed and apparently deserted tent. They were about to peer into it when a radio began to play. Lest they be accused of intruding, the three boys stole away.

'I wonder if it was Harry Roberts?' one of them suggested when he got home. Angry with him for getting wet when he had a cold, his mother doused his childish enthusiasm with adult contempt. 'That's impossible', she snapped.

Once again Roberts had escaped detection; but this time through no fault of his own. Far from being warier as autumn made him more vulnerable, he was growing more complacent than ever, having added a small stolen stove and a makeshift chimney to the comforts of his already too comfortable home.

On October 21 he read that Duddy and Witney were to stand trial at the Old Bailey on November 14. Roberts had hidden like an animal in the forest, yet shopped in the village each day like an innocent housewife. His camp was so sited and constructed as to escape attention perhaps forever; yet once inside his tent he had regularly turned on his transistor radio and lit his lantern. Hell bent on evading capture, he had bought leather for a quite unnecessary holster from a tanner whose premises were directly opposite those of the local police station. Devoid of any remorse for the crime he had committed, or for the families of the men he had murdered, he went to considerable pains, while awaiting trial, to write Witney a letter, the implication of which was that Witney had masterminded the crime itself.

The 'Fund-Raising Party'

One night Jack Slipper was duty officer in the special operations room when he had a call from an officer saying that he had heard there was a party that night in a public house to raise funds for Roberts' defence and there could be as many as 300 people attending. That is the kind of event that just has to be raided. Apart from finding out who Roberts' close associates were, there was a real possibility that the police might just find Roberts himself here. Bravado is very important in the criminal fraternity and it would not have been at all unlikely for Roberts to have looked in for half-an-hour to collect a round of applause.

It was very short notice to raise a team for that kind of raid, but Slipper managed to round up 30 officers. The function was supposed to be at a pub called the *Prince of Wales* in Notting Hill, but he kept his men well clear until he was quite sure the party really was going on. You can look a real idiot barging into a bar with 30 policemen only to find you're dealing with half-a-dozen casual drinkers.

The publican was well respected by the locals and though Slipper did not know him personally, he had the man described to him and went in to have a chat. The public bar was quiet and so was the saloon, but from upstairs you could hear music and the sounds of a fair-sized crowd, and he guessed that he was on the right track. He talked to the publican and confirmed that it was a fund-raising do at a 'Flim-a-Head' (£5 each), but he did not know who it was for.

That was enough and Slipper called in ten officers, leaving the rest to cover the exits. They went upstairs and found a long, crowded room with a four-piece band and a singer on a rostrum at one end. As soon as they went in, the singer spotted them and announced 'the attendance of the Old Bill'. Then the fun started. The crowd at this kind of do is always pretty lively. It was the usual crew of publicans, bookmakers, criminals, and people who just like to associate with criminals, hangers-on who know that villains are often free spenders.

That kind of crowd does not like to be seen to be meek in front of the police. They usually make some noise at first, then when they see that the police are there in numbers and that there is no point in getting into difficulties they go quiet and cold, especially if the police are armed. At one point, Slipper felt a hand in his pocket. He grabbed it; it was the organizer's. 'Look, Guvnor,' he said, 'I'm sorry to tell you this, but someone has just put a lighted cigarette in your pocket'. Slipper thought he was trying to have him over and was about to make a show of charging the man with attempted larceny, just to show that the police could not be pushed around, when a drunken woman nearby admitted she had done it. Slipper let it pass, as by that time they had the situation under control; the police had shut down the music and started questioning some of the organizers.

METROPOLITAN POLICE

£1,000 REWARD

MURDER

A reward or rewards up to a total of £1,000 will be paid for information leading to the arrest of HARRY MAURICE ROBERTS, b. Wanstead, Essex, on 21-7-36, 5ft. 10in., photo. above, wanted for questioning in connection with the murder of three police officers on the 12th August, 1966, at Braybrook Street, Shepherds Bush.

Information to be given to New Scotland Yard, S.W.1, or at any police station.

The amount of any payment will be in the discretion of the Commissioner of Police for the Metropolis.

J. SIMPSON,
Commissioner of Police.

Reward poster

It was a fund-raising party, but not for Harry Roberts. Still, Slipper did not feel too bad about the raid because it turned out they were raising funds for a well-known south London villain who at the time was remanded in custody charged with attempting to murder another police officer, after a car chase in Bromley. In the six weeks after the shooting the special operations room at The Bush received more than 6,000 calls from the public about sightings of Harry Roberts. There were sometimes as many as 30 raiding parties sent out to respond to these calls. Every call was followed up by the police. They worked to keep the momentum up with broadcasts on TV and radio, articles in the press and 16,000 posters placed offering a reward of £1,000 for Roberts' capture.

However, it was not until mid-November, three months after the murders, that he was found. His discovery coincided dramatically with the opening of the trial of Witney and Duddy on Monday 15 November at the Old Bailey. Chitty was sitting listening to evidence when the news was whispered to him.

Tracing the Source of the Guns

In September, whilst Roberts was still on the run, the investigation ran out of leads for Slipper to investigate and he was tasked by Chitty and Hensley with identifying and tracing the man who had sold the guns to Roberts. They already knew, from Lillian Perry (with whom Roberts' had lodged), that Roberts had bought three guns from a Cypriot, for £90. They also knew that gun running was quiet common in the Greek (and Greek Cypriot) community and that the weapons were usually shipped in as components with other goods and then assembled in England.

Mrs Perry told the officers that she had driven from Bristol, with Roberts, in his Daimler, in February or March 1966, to a meeting place in the West End. They met the man with the guns in a 'triangle-shaped café' somewhere in London. She said there were three guns, one looked like a Luger, another was smaller and lighter, and looked like a toy gun, and that a certain amount of ammunition was included in the package deal.

For weeks, while Slipper was trailing around camping shops and observing Roberts' mother by day, he was spending the nights in the 'spielers' of Camden Town where the Greeks and Greek Cypriots enjoyed themselves until the early hours. A spieler is a place where cards and dice are played. Greeks love to gamble and when they have finished eating or drinking and dancing for the evening, they go on to a spieler — usually a room rented for £100 a week or so — and gamble the rest of the night away.

There is no point in a six foot three inch Flying Squad officer with a British military-style moustache trying to work undercover in the Greek community. Slipper had to get himself invited in and the best way to do that was through a local CID officer who really knew his manor. Once inside, Slipper could get close to the owner of the club and exert some pressure to get information, because 'spieling' is technically illegal. He had to show that he was a reasonable sort of copper and that he was not planning to use a heavy hammer to crack down on what they saw as a normal community recreation. But at the same time, he made it clear that they would have the police on their back until he found the criminal that he was looking for.

Slowly, the investigation started to make progress. The detectives received an anonymous telephone call informing them that another Cypriot had acted as the middle-man, and had introduced Roberts to a man called Costas, who supplied the guns to Roberts. So keen had Roberts been to buy that he met the middle-man in a café behind the *Moulin Rouge* restaurant, off Shaftesbury Avenue, not far from Piccadilly Circus. This man was found, after many weeks, but it was no easy task. Detectives raided gambling clubs all over London in order to identify the middle man, who they knew to be an inveterate gambler. Then one night he was seen to leave a club in Swiss Cottage, and they tailed him to a newsagent's shop in Pratt Street in an area of Camden Town known as Little Cyprus, that belonged to the supplier of the weapons, a man they now knew to be Christos Costas.

Costas was a Cypriot, six foot tall and weighing 18 stone. He was known locally as 'Big Alcos'. Slipper got a warrant to search the newsagent's shop, and the flat above it. He had received a tip that Roberts might be hiding there but a thorough search satisfied them that he was not, and Costas was able to satisfy the officers that he had never been there. He was telling the truth, but he neglected to tell the officers that he had met Roberts in February or March 1966 and sold him the guns that he and Duddy had used to kill the detectives.

Slipper took six officers to raid the shop at 5.30 in the morning. Costas was a massive man, tall with broad shoulders, and very aggressive. When the officers entered the shop on the warrant, he was laying out piles of newspapers to sell, and he really turned on them. He started screaming that the officers had no right to interrupt his business and threatened to throw them all out of the shop. The officers would not normally have had any problem in calming him down, but just as they were getting ready to restrain him, a tipper lorry drew up outside the shop and 20 Irish labourers entered the shop to buy their morning papers and cigarettes on the way to work, and the newsagent started a tremendous scene when the officers tried to keep them out. He went on about how they were trying to ruin him and the labourers quickly got into the spirit of the thing and started insisting on being served.

Nevertheless, Slipper quickly regained control of the situation by sending a woman officer upstairs to get Costas' wife out of bed so that she could run the shop. He subdued Costas and eventually arrested him.

When the search was completed the officers conveyed Costas to The Bush and there he became calm and quiet. Instead of yelling and screaming, he sat back casually and said, 'OK, so I did supply the guns. I didn't know they were going to be used in a murder'. He smiled and shrugged: 'In England, possessing guns is nothing. What can I get? Three months? Six months? So why should I care? Sure. I admit it'.

Early in February 1967, Costas was charged and appeared at Bow Street Magistrate's Court, accused of selling Roberts the three guns, a .38 Colt Special, a 9 mm Luger and .38 Enfield. There were also four other charges of being in unlawful possession of firearms and ammunition, and not having the necessary firearms certificates. He was committed, on bail, for trial at the Inner London Sessions and, it was alleged, that when he had been charged he told Det Supt Chitty, 'I plead guilty. This means three months at the most. I am not worried'.

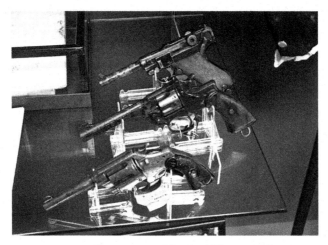

The guns used by the killers
© Metropolitan Police Museum

In April, Costas appeared in the dock and having taken legal advice and considered his position, he pleaded 'not guilty' to all charges. Harry Roberts appeared at court as a witness in a charcoal grey suit, handcuffed to two policemen. He had been allowed to change out of his blue prison uniform with a broad yellow stripe, indicating he was a potential escape risk, so as not to prejudice the jury against him and his testimony. He had travelled up to London from the security wing at Parkhurst Prison, with a strong escort of police and a helicopter hovering overhead all the way, until he was securely lodged in Wandsworth Gaol.

All that day, Roberts stayed in a cell below the court as Lillian Perry gave evidence. She told the court how she had driven with Roberts to a place near the *Moulin Rouge*, and she had watched him meet Costas. She told of a conversation between the two men in the back of a car, that she handed £90 in notes to Roberts, and that he in turn handed them to Costas. The actual transaction took place on the corner of Denmark Street ('Tin Pan Alley' of song-writing fame) and Charing Cross Road. It was clear that Roberts knew how much he had to pay for he had given the money to Mrs Perry previously. She also told how Costas showed Roberts how the guns worked.

At the end of the day, when the court adjourned, Roberts was taken back to Wandsworth under heavy escort. The next day he was called into the witness box for the defence. Three prison officers stood close, and the court and public gallery were full of detectives who had been on the original manhunt. Roberts, looking a little thinner than when he had appeared at the Old Bailey, seemed to be enjoying the situation. He looked all around at the packed court and clearly derived considerable satisfaction from being the centre of attention again. So tight was the security that no-one was allowed to enter or leave the court while Roberts (who had by this time already started his sentence) was in the witness box, probably due to the fact that soon after arriving in prison he had told people that he intended to escape at the first opportunity.

In evidence, Roberts admitted that he had committed many offences and that the last offence was the most grave. He agreed with the prosecuting counsel that the shooting of three policemen at Shepherd's Bush was 'the most appalling crime'. And then he said he had never seen Costas in his life before, and he said it without a blush or any change in his expression. He bought the guns, he said, from a man in south London, somewhere near the Old Kent Road, and, he added, 'I would be putting this man in the dock if I said who he was. I will not tell you who he is, or what his business is.

'I arrived at a turning off the Old Kent Road with Mrs Perry. I left her in the car and went off to meet this man. I completed this transaction with him and he drove me back to my car and I got into it. He also got in and we discussed a few things with Mrs Perry, and he went away, and I went away'.

Joseph Yahuda, defending Costas, referred to 'Mr Roberts', which caused Reginald Seaton, the chairman of the court, to interrupt him and say, 'Call him "Roberts" please. He is a murderer'. Yehuda replied, 'I think that we should show respect to people...' Seaton said, 'Please do not argue. Call him "Roberts" in future'. Yahuda said, 'As your Lordship pleases'. Yahuda then asked Roberts, 'Do you know anything about guns, or were these new to you?' Roberts said, 'I was in the Army'.

'Not only were you not born yesterday, you know something about crime?'

'A little'.

'In your nightmares would you go to buy guns in the West End?'

'It would not be a logical place to transact any business in guns'.

Roberts admitted to prosecuting counsel, John Mathew, that two of the guns he bought were with him when he was arrested, and that he had been seen in Wandsworth Prison by Det Supt Chitty.

Mathew asked him, 'That was one occasion when, I suggest, you used the expression "grass". Do you remember?'

'Probably, but the interview was obtained by false pretences'.

Roberts admitted that he had been shown statements made by Lillian Perry and by Costas, but he denied that he said, 'What Lil has said is right, but I'm not going to say any more'.

He also denied that he had said to Chitty, 'You have been very fair with me and you will get him down without me. He did me a favour and I can't grass on him. I am not grassing on them, even if they are Greek'.

Roberts appeared to enjoy being in the witness box. He smiled frequently and was completely composed. There was little doubt that the jury of nine men and three women believed the evidence of Mrs Perry and that of the detectives. They clearly did not believe Roberts. They took an hour to reach their verdict of guilty on all three counts: selling Roberts the three handguns; possessing the weapons without a firearms certificate; and having a Colt pistol and ammunition in Denmark Street in Soho. Achilles Antoniades, defending, said, 'It is impossible for anyone in this court to erase from his mind what happened on that tragic day in August last year. But I would like the court to accept that this simple, this uneducated, friendly and fundamentally good-hearted man would never have allowed himself, if he had known, to get involved in a case like this for all the gold in the world'.

The chairman, Reginald Seaton, took a very different view. He said, 'This is a classic example of the danger of people who transact matters concerning firearms in the criminal world … It is quite apparent that when you went into this you knew quite clearly what was likely to happen. At your door, indirectly, lay the deaths of three courageous policemen. I cannot help but take a serious view of these offences'.

Costas was given three years for illegally possessing the guns, and three years for selling them to Roberts, to run consecutively. He was sentenced to another three years, to run concurrently, for possessing firearms in a public place. Clearly, he was not as knowledgeable on English law as he thought, because hearing that he had received a total of six years imprisonment left him looking seriously shaken when the sentence was handed down.

Roberts still appeared to be unconcerned. Perhaps he felt he had done his duty by denying that he knew Costas, which he may have thought would enhance his reputation in prison as a man who did not betray fellow criminals. His last words, as he left court to be taken back to prison, were to a detective. He said, 'See you when I'm 68'.

CHAPTER 6

John Witney and John Duddy

John Edward Witney

John Edward Witney was the leader of the gang of robbers, having shown himself to be brighter than Harry Roberts and good at selecting suitable victims for their robberies, although Roberts' penchant for violence and using firearms had recently made him a growing influence in the gang. The third man, Duddy, had only joined the gang a few weeks earlier and had yet to establish his position.

Born in 1930, Witney was described by a young witness at his trial as resembling Bobby Charlton, a star of the England soccer team that had recently won the 1966 World Cup Final. At the time of the robbery, Witney lived with his wife in a flat in Fernhead Road in Paddington. Roberts frequently visited Witney there to discuss their future crimes. He would speak with enthusiasm about the advantage of taking firearms out to work and Witney's wife would become agitated and threaten to leave her husband if he continued to work with Roberts. While most criminals saw Roberts as dangerous and refused to work with him, Witney's was all for using weapons.

Witney was also the gang's driver and had driven them around as they committed their robberies, but he had not shot any of the officers and was convicted on the basis of entering into a joint enterprise by agreeing to go out to commit robbery knowing that his accomplices were in possession of firearms. This made him equally guilty as his two fellow gang members who had actually shot the officers, but meant that he derived a certain sympathy from ignorant people who did not understand this vital principle of English law, which regarded him also as one of the killers of the policemen.

At his trial at the Old Bailey, Witney was sentenced to life imprisonment, with a recommendation that he serve at least 30 years, and avoided receiving the death penalty which had been removed from the statute book just eight months earlier. However, the trial judge told all three of the accused that this was 'the most heinous crime' in a generation and warned him and his two accomplices that they might never be freed.

Witney's release in 1991 caused considerable controversy, as he had served just 25 years of the 30 year tariff for the shootings that had been set by the trial judge. He had also become the first police killer in history to be released from prison, most of the others having been hanged.

On Monday 16 August 1999 Witney, then aged 69, was found dead, lying in a pool of blood in his flat in Douglas Road, Horfield, Bristol. A post mortem examination revealed that he had suffered horrific head injuries and then been throttled to death.

His flatmate, Nigel Evans, a 38-year-old heroin addict later appeared before Bristol Crown Court charged with his murder. The court was told that he had a history of minor crime and that both men had been sent to live at the flat upon their release from prison. At first, Evans and Witney got on well, but Evans had a heroin habit which led to him running up rent arrears of £750. The two men then rowed over the debt and the daily household chores, such as washing-up. Evans beat Witney around the head with a hammer and grabbed him by the throat. Witney, who by then was quite frail, was throttled to death.

Evans was found unanimously guilty and sentenced to life imprisonment. Gaoling him, Mrs Justice Smith told him: 'It is my view that there was much more behind the way in which this dispute arose than you have told us'. Police ruled out any connection between his murder and the events of 1966. Det Ch Insp Mike Hems of Avon and Somerset Police said: 'We are investigating the murder here, as opposed to the events in 1966. There is no connection with his convictions in 1966'.

John Duddy

John Duddy, the second shooter, was born in Glasgow on 27 December 1928. He was five feet five inches tall and of medium build, slightly corpulent with a fresh complexion, light brown hair, blue eyes and scars on the top of his right forefinger and both knees. He had a tattoo on his right forearm of a pierced skull and heart with the words, 'True to Death'. When last seen, before the shooting, he had been wearing dark trousers and a dark patterned, probably striped, pullover.

Until six weeks before the shootings in Shepherd's Bush, Duddy had been driving a lorry, but when Witney and Roberts decided that they needed a third member for their gang they invited Duddy to join them. Roberts had strong views in favour of using firearms in the robberies that they committed on rent collectors, bookmakers, post offices, building societies and banks and he was happy to spread them widely. Many professional criminals refused to work with him for this very reason, but Duddy had made it clear that he shared these views and this probably secured his selection.

Duddy hailed from the Gorbals district of Glasgow and came before the courts at the age of 13, for stealing a bicycle. It was not long before he again appeared in front of a juvenile court for theft and then, early in 1945, he was sent to borstal for two years for housebreaking. Within weeks of being released he received his first prison sentence of three months for stealing, which was quickly followed by another three months for another theft. His last conviction had been in Scotland in May 1948, following which he had to serve six months imprisonment for stealing.

Many young men become involved in crime when they are young, but desist as they grow up, get married and start a family. This was the case with Duddy, who went on to spend 18 years free of any convictions, and this had persuaded police that he was no longer concerned in crime. Exactly what drove him back to his previous ways is not clear. It may have been financial difficulties or domestic problems. It was strange that this wayward and weak-willed youth should have had for his father a Glasgow city policeman but, at least, until the day of the murders, he had never been known to use violence. He had moved to London after marrying a local girl from near his home and then became a long-distance lorry driver, making the occasional visit to his old friends in Glasgow, as and when his job required.

Some months before the shootings, in August, he had begun to drink heavily and started mixing with a set of people who frequented the dimly-lit clubs of west London, around Notting Hill, Chelsea and Fulham. It was in one of these clubs, *La Monde*, that he was introduced to Roberts and Witney. The lady who brought about the introduction was Mrs June Howard, who was Roberts' landlady at the time of the shooting, and who, with her husband, was a witness at Roberts' wedding to his strip-tease dancer wife, Margaret.

Duddy was still serving the term of 30 years' imprisonment, imposed for the Braybrook Street Massacre, when he died in the hospital at Parkhurst Prison on the Isle of Wight on Sunday 8 February 1981.

CHAPTER 7

Harry Roberts: This Is Your Life

'Have you seen this man?' Metropolitan Police Service handout, 1966

'Height 5ft 10 in, slimmish built, slightly sunken cheeks, quiff of hair in centre of forehead that falls down frequently, George Robey eyebrows, left side of mouth twists up slightly, a big eater, drinks little and then brown or light ale, or Coca Cola, has a passion for suede shoes, occasionally takes purple hearts, smokes tipped cigarettes fairly heavily, spends freely and gambles sometimes, has scars over his left eye and under the right eyelid, appendix, and a small scar on the base of the right thumb, has long fingers and bites his nails, slightly protruding teeth, needs to shave only occasionally.'

This is the photograph and description of Harry Roberts that the Metropolitan Police were quickly able to release to the media and the public when John Witney named him as his accomplice in the Braybrook Street Massacre the day after the crime. It was sufficient to allow any public-minded citizen to identify Roberts and report his sighting to the police; the public must have thought so because in the 96 days that Roberts was on the run the more than 6,000 sightings of 'him' were reported.

However, after a few days, with Witney and Duddy charged and locked up in police custody, when no sign could be found of Roberts, Chitty and Hensley realised that they did not know enough about Roberts' lifestyle, his friends and the places that he frequented, and detectives were tasked with investigating Roberts' life. They prepared a file that became known as the 'This Is Your Life' file, after the BBC TV show then hosted by Eamonn Andrews that ran from 1955 until 1964, and again from 1969 until to 1987. These detectives would have picked up Roberts' Criminal Records Office (CRO) file, the correspondence relating to his previous arrests, and spoken to police officers, prison officers, school teachers, friends, etc. who knew him.

Harry Roberts was born in Wanstead Essex on Tuesday 21 July 1935 to Harry and Dorothy Roberts, who managed *The George* public house at 155–159, High St, London E11. His father was the cellarman and his mother the bar manager. Although the pub's address places it in Wanstead High Street, it is actually a large Edwardian pub on the corner of the main A12 highway and next to Wanstead Underground Station. Wanstead is on the north side of the Dagenham/Walthamstow line that separates the East End Docklands in the south from the more pretentious north side of Essex, such as Woodford, Chigwell and Theydon Bois.

Pretentious or not, Dorothy Roberts was seriously involved in crime. She stole, received stolen goods, and dealt in the black market in order to defeat the rationing that was introduced to deal with the lack of food and luxuries brought about by the Second World War. Her position as a publican gave her ready access to the thieves, rogues, vagabonds and dealers with whom she wanted to do business.

It was into this 'family business' that the young Harry was introduced at an early age. A close relationship developed between Harry and his mother, that was to persist through until her death, and which inspired Dorothy to assist Harry in many of his 22 escape bids from prison. By the time Harry was seven years-of-age his parents had split up and left the pub, and young Harry was sent to St Joseph's College in West Norwood, near Crystal Palace. St Joseph's was a Roman Catholic school for boys founded in 1855. The school had, and still has, a proud academic, sporting and disciplinary reputation and counts among its alumni two former Lord Mayors of London, Sir William Dunn and Sir John Gilbert.

During the school holidays, Roberts returned to stay with his mother and to assist her in the family business. When he was 13, he made strenuous objections to having to be a border at the school and his mother allowed him to revert to being a day boy there, no doubt relieved at not having to pay the considerable boarding fees. He went back to live with her. A few months later, his behaviour led to him being expelled from St Joseph's and sent to another school in the same area. After only a few more months, just before he reached the age of 15, he was expelled from the second school. After his this, he took a series of jobs as a carpenter, a porter, an electrician's mate, a street trader and a lorry driver. However, he continued with his criminal enterprises. When he was 18 in August 1954 he was convicted of assault with intent to rob a shopkeeper with an iron bar and sentenced to borstal training and was sent to Gaynes Hall Borstal near Huntingdon in Cambridgeshire until 3rd January 1956.

Just a week after his release, on 11 January 1956 Roberts was called up for National Service and joined the Rifle Brigade (Prince Consort's Own), with whom he saw action during the Kenyan (Mau Mau) Uprising and the Malayan Emergency. Of his service in the jungle he said that this was where he learned to kill and that he had 'personally killed at least four'. Roberts has claimed that he reached the rank of sergeant while in the army although others have given his rank as lance corporal.

Former 'Public Enemy Number One', armed robber turned sociologist and journalist, John McVicar, has said that Roberts 'gloated' about his killings while in prison, and that he claimed to have 'acquired a taste for killing prisoners-of-war on the orders of his officers'. On 17 March 1958 he left the Army upon completing his National Service. He was a good mechanic and soon got a job as a driver, and on 3 March 1958 he married Margaret Rose at St Pancras Registry Office. The witnesses were Mr and Mrs Colin Howard, the same people he stayed with during the weeks before the murders. For a while the couple lived with his mother and were happy together, but domestic rows, almost inevitable in a small flat shared by people of different temperaments, led to them finding a place of their own. His mother visited them frequently, and, eventually, persuaded them to return to her but when the rows flared up they moved away again.

His weekly wage at that time was £7 14s 1d as a warehouseman, and his wife was earning £8 a week as a barmaid. But shortly before Christmas he was sacked for what was described as 'irregularities'. These, in fact, were a charge of store-breaking and theft from the warehouse where he worked. Once again, he was in the dock, this time at Essex Quarter Sessions, at Chelmsford, and he was sentenced to 21 months' imprisonment. It was then that his wife learned about his previous convictions.

When he was found guilty, the judge, as is customary, asked, 'Is there anything known?' (Does this man have any previous convictions?) The detective inspector replied in the affirmative and Mrs Roberts heard the melancholy facts of her husband's past ... the probation, the National Service, the casual work usually at an average wage of between £3 and £4 a week.

There had been one bright spot in the inspector's evidence — Roberts' Army testimonial, from the Infantry Record Office at Exeter, read:

'Hard working and conscientious, capable of working without supervision. Loyal and has a pleasing manner and is strongly recommended to a future employer.'

Nevertheless, having been found guilty, he was sentenced to imprisonment. He walked down the steps between two prison officers to begin his first real custodial sentence and was sent to Maidstone Prison. His wife, alone after such a short period of marriage, continued to visit him and worked to keep their home together, but all the time she was nursing a guilty secret. In the weeks since their marriage, she had taken Roberts to visit an old man who had been a family friend for many years most

Sunday afternoons. Then two men had posed as tax inspectors in order to gain entry into the man's home. Once inside, the man had been bound and robbed and beaten about the head with a heavy glass decanter. The robbers cut off the old man's finger in order to steal his wedding ring. The old man never recovered from the injuries that were inflicted on him that day and died a year and three days after the incident. Mrs Roberts put the pieces together:

> 'I knew then. I faced Harry with it and he admitted it. He told me he had taken the ring off the old man's finger. He and the other man went to the pictures that night. I didn't know what to do, I was his wife, after all.'

Soon Flying Squad officers visited Roberts in prison to see what he knew about the incident in Burma Road just off Green Lanes in Stoke Newington and on 23 March 1959 Roberts appeared at the Old Bailey charged with robbery and was convicted and sentenced to seven years' imprisonment, on top of the term that he was already serving. As the law then stood, if the old man had died two days earlier (within a year and one day rather than a year and three days) then he could have been charged with murder and at a time when the death penalty was still in force. The judge, Mr Justice Maude, made reference to the fact that Roberts had so narrowly avoided this fate, saying: 'You are a brutal thug. You came very near the rope this time. It is to be hoped you do not appear before us again'. He would be back before the same court within six years in connection with the murder of the three detectives in Shepherd's Bush. His wife later said, 'I next saw him at the Old Bailey. I was seven-and-a-half months pregnant at the time. When they sentenced him to seven years, he swore he would get me for shopping him'.

So, at the age of 22, the brutality Roberts had concealed behind a grin and twinkling eyes from his fellow soldiers in Malaya, was revealed to the Central Criminal Court. His wife watched him being led away. It was the last time she saw him. 'Everything suddenly went black,' she said, 'and I woke up in an ambulance on my way to hospital. Soon afterwards I knew I had lost my baby'.

He was conveyed to Pentonville Prison in a Black Maria (prison van). The old fortress-type gaol in north London is the first stop for all offenders convicted of any offence and sentenced to imprisonment north of the River Thames. For Roberts, like all the other new arrivals, this was a period of being kept under observation so that his behaviour could be assessed and a decision made as to where he would serve the remainder of his sentence.

Although Roberts had been previously convicted, he behaved so well that, after a few months, the authorities re-classified him as a 'first offender'. This meant that he could be posted to a prison which catered for men whom it was felt would react to humane treatment and training, with a view to being completely rehabilitated. No-one will ever know whether this was a good or bad decision, as there is no way of telling what goes on in the human mind when a man is locked up for long periods. Roberts was considered to be the right material, so instead of going to Dartmoor, once described by a Home Secretary as 'a cesspit of humanity', which is a prison for men sentenced to five years or more, he was sent to Wormwood Scrubs, classified as a 'star' prison for first offenders.

Most of his time in there was spent in a single cell on D-Wing. When he first arrived, after he had showered and been given his suit of navy-blue battle-dress, he was ordered to scrub out a particularly filthy cell. He had no option but to comply, as to disobey any order in prison is a punishable offence, but he told other prisoners that he resented having to clear up another person's mess. Never again did he scrub his cell, a gesture against authority of which he boasted. Apart from that, he was neat and tidy in his dress and appearance, and when he qualified for certain privileges, his mother sent him an expensive red carpet to lay in his cell. Roberts always stubbed out his cigarettes and pushed them under the carpet, another petty gesture which he thought gave him some status as a rebel.

It was during his time that Roberts' sexuality started to attract attention. Many young men who have developed unusually close relationships with their mothers, go on to become homosexuals, and a considerable amount of scientific research has investigated the relationship between homosexual men and their mothers. Roberts has shown no such tendencies, but does appear to have issues with developing sexual relationships with women. Prison officers frequently reported that Roberts regularly masturbated in the same way that other prisoners have did, and that, whilst detained at Wormwood Scrubs as a young man, he went to the trouble of manufacturing a home-made periscope, with which he was able to look into the nearby nurses home in the evenings when the prison staff extinguished all lights at 9 pm. The nurses, of course, returned to the home after late turn, and would get undressed in front of their open windows, unaware of the attention being paid to them. Roberts even joined with other prisoners to design a method of communicating with his fellow prisoners to alert them to the presence of a young nurse undressing in the nurses home, so that a nurse standing naked in front of a window on the fifth floor at the third window from the left induced a signal of five taps on the water pipe followed by three taps on the water pipe, followed by a long break, before it was repeated. The two women with whom Roberts formed relationships in the short time that he has not been locked up in prison were surprised that he flashed his cash and bought them expensive presents, shared their beds, but never made any physical demands of them and rejected any advances that they made.

As with most prisoners, Roberts teamed up with a few like-minded individuals, with whom he spent his leisure time. In his case he was a member of a gang of four who stuck together throughout all the varying vicissitudes of prison life. In the evenings and at weekends they played cards — whist, bridge, poker and brag — and at all these games, Roberts was quite proficient, although he lacked patience. He would stay quiet for hours while the games were played or whilst a discussion on some topic or other was going on around him. Then, with the electrifying suddenness of summer lighting, he would erupt and try to crush all other arguments by the sheer power of his voice, with a liberal sprinkling of four letter words.

On these occasions, his eyes bulged, and became glazed and hostile. His companions always felt that violence was not far away, but mostly they managed to calm him down. Sometimes he was extremely violent, throwing his cards down on the table, and after pushing his chair back so hard that it crashed to the floor, he would stride away and go to his cell. That was usually a sure sign that he would sulk for a whole week, refusing to speak to anyone but the prison officers, and only then when asked a direct question. When he recovered from his sulking he was perfectly normal and quickly regained his popularity.

In prison the two most popular subjects for discussion are sex and the 'big job' to be organized on release. Roberts was as boastful as the other young men about his sexual prowess, although his drawings and paintings revealed a distrust of women that amounted to nothing less than sexual aversion. All his female contacts seemed to be either as bland as Walt Disney's *Snow White* or as predatory as the *Wicked Queen*. Roberts' main artistic obsession was in fact not the female form but an exploding ship sinking into a sea of flames. There appears to be little evidence of his success with women.

He did sometimes talk of planning a successful coup which would bring him a fortune in cash with no chance of being arrested. But his passion was always guns. Roberts had to move away from his usual gang in order to talk about guns because none of those guys had any time for using firearms in their criminal pursuits, so he found three other men who shared his enthusiasm for the subject. Roberts was an expert, calling on his experience in Malaya and the fact that he was an army marksman with both the rifle and the Bren gun; the others had also received some weapon training during their National Service.

These talks were to lead to disaster for three of them, and to the deaths of four innocent men. One of the quartet took part in an armed hold-up and was sent back to prison, but is now free again so he cannot be named. Another, a great friend of Roberts, was one Joseph Martin, a labourer by trade, who was no stranger to gaol.

When Roberts was released from prison in November 1963, he went to lodge at Mrs Lillian Perry's terraced house in Filton Grove, Horfield, Bristol and worked as a bricklayer on a Wimpey housing development site at Weston-Super-Mare, in Somerset. Workmates say he drove himself to the limit to earn as much overtime and bonus money as possible, sometimes making as much as £70 per week.

One of his neighbours, Frederick Holbrook, said, 'Roberts was a good neighbour when he lived next door. I lent him my car when his own broke down. He returned it to me each weekend with the tank full to the brim. When his own came back he wanted to pay me hire money for using mine. I refused so he ran it down to a local garage and had two new tyres fitted'.

The car Roberts had was a second-hand Daimler which he bought for £650. It was used as one of the bridal cars when Mrs Perry's daughter was married, with Roberts driving, wearing a borrowed chauffeur's cap and dark glasses. The reason for this subterfuge was that Mrs Perry was anxious that her husband should not find out about her relationship with Roberts when he attended the wedding. Roberts reassured her, 'I'll be there, but he won't notice me'. So as one of the chauffeurs he was asked in, and was able to mingle with the guests.

After a few months' bricklaying, Roberts decided to go into the sub-contracting business, organizing a team of men, which he took around building sites in a second-hand van he bought. In one six-month period, he cleared £1,800 for himself; he worked hard, but spent on the grand scale at weekends, taking out Mrs Perry and other friends to expensive restaurants. One bank holiday he took her all the way to John O'Groats, and was back in good time to begin work on the Tuesday.

And then, just as it seemed that Roberts would prove one of the finest success stories of the prison rehabilitation scheme, he suddenly lost interest. The credit squeeze had made things a little more difficult, but there was still plenty of money to be picked up. Perhaps Roberts had been living in the 'sticks' too long, and was pining for London, for in March 1966, he decided to leave Bristol. He also left behind several hire-purchase debts and a sizeable overdraft at a Bristol bank. Mrs Perry went with him, leaving her husband and married daughter at Filton Grove.

Eight months before Roberts became a murderer, his friend Martin teamed up with four other men to embark on his big criminal enterprise. At half=past-five one afternoon the five men, wearing nylon stocking masks and armed with a shotgun, a revolver and iron bars, burst into the cashier's office at United Dairies, in Wood Green in north London. The deputy manager of the depot, Alfred Philo, who lived on the premises, was alerted and ran across the yard to cut off the escape of the bandits. He was shot. As he lay dying, the gang jumped into their stolen car to escape. But, in their absence another car had parked in front of them, and such was their panic, they rammed it before backing off and driving away. The driver of the parked car happened to be a schoolteacher who was still sitting in the front seat, and she saw the face of the bandit driver in her mirror. Philo was a devoted family man and he died in Christmas week. At the time, his widow said, 'He loved his two grandchildren and was looking forward to spending the holiday with them. We had their presents already packed'. It was another shooting murder which left tragedy in its cruel wake.

Joseph Martin, who was then aged 32, was arrested by Det Supt Sidney Bradbury, who, like Jack Slipper, was another former Flying Squad officer who had been involved in the investigation into the Great Train Robbery. Martin stood trial with the other four. The prosecution claimed that it was Martin who had fired the fatal shot and the jury found him guilty. He was sentenced to life imprisonment for murder and 16 years for robbing the dairy of £886; three of the others were sent to prison and the fourth man was found not guilty of being an accessory and discharged.

Since men who have been in gaol invariably follow the fortunes of their fellows, and since there is no censorship of newspapers, it is reasonable to suppose that Roberts read about the case and was aware of the fate of his erstwhile cell-mate. If he did, it made little difference, for guns remained his favourite subject.

In Wormwood Scrubs, as in most other prisons, the business of bookmaking goes on in quite an astonishing fashion. At that time there were two rival factions, who more or less shared the punters' investments. Currency for placing bets, or for winning payments, was tobacco, known as 'snout' in prison language, which was worth five shillings an ounce. Roberts took no part in this, although many of his friends were ringleaders. He was prepared to support them in times of trouble but was never known to have a bet, having no interest in horse racing or in football. He was not concerned with winning tobacco because, whilst most of the prisoners smoked cigarettes which they rolled them from Old Holborn tobacco, he bought a cheaper brand, known as Black Beauty, which was stocked in the canteen and which most men would smoke only in dire emergency. Similarly, while many men bought chocolate, or extra foods, and small luxuries from their meagre wages, he contented himself with the ordinary prison fare. He was fortunate in his time at Wormwood Scrubs to have as the Governor, Gilbert Hair, who was a visionary in prison affairs. He had a passionate belief in reforming prison organization away from the old concepts of the convict days of regulations and brutality. He wanted prison to be a place of genuine rehabilitation, where time was not wasted on pointless and stupid tasks so that a man might take his freedom with courage, and hope for an honest future.

Roberts benefitted from this and soon after he arrived there he became a 'blue band', a trusty prisoner, allowed to escort parties of up to 12 men to their tasks. He also took a course in bricklaying and worked at it with fierce concentration. Prisoners tell how he stayed in his cell for hours at a time, studying text books and drawing sections of houses and walls. His determination was so strong that he allowed nothing to distract him from his purpose, which was to gain him his certificate from the City and Guilds examining board, finishing at the top of his class. Then he took a course in plumbing and passed that too. His popularity grew at that time because he learned more easily than most of the class, and he was prepared to help others with their problems.

He was, by now, entitled to more privileges: he had curtains at his cell window and a powerful radio set. Among his friends was an electronics engineer who devised a scheme to relay the radio programmes from Roberts' set to the cells of those who were not entitled to have one. The charge was half an ounce of tobacco a month and all that was required was a needle, a telephone ear-piece and two pieces of wire. The wire and needle were obtained from one of the workshops and the ear-piece from the shop where old GPO equipment was dismantled so that the more expensive parts could be used again.

The programmes were relayed through the electrical bell system which runs from cell-to-cell allowing prisoners to summon assistance in an emergency. The two wires were connected to the ear-piece and then onto the heat pipe, for an earth, and the other to the needle which was plugged into the bell push. Roberts merely had to plug his set into the bell-push for all the men on the circuit to hear the programmes. So successful was this scheme that at one time more than 200 men were enjoying a radio service to which they were not entitled. But like so many schemes hatched in prison, it was discovered. Some men, who got behind in their payments and were asked to pay up, turned sour and turned informant. Roberts was caught and his radio was confiscated.

His mother was a regular visitor and Roberts looked forward to these occasions, especially in the summer months when he could sit with her at a table on the edge of the cricket field and buy her tea and cakes. He had no other visitors but would sometimes see the friends or relatives of other prisoners who, for one reason or another, were unable to keep their appointments. On those occasions he would pass on whatever messages were left and all the news of the man's family.

In the tiny punishment cell, which prisoners call 'chokey', in Wormwood Scrubs prison, a young man called Harry Roberts sat in dreadful solitude. He had been there for days, alone for 23 hours out of 24, with no books or papers to read, no materials to write or paint. The cell was empty but for a chamber pot, a bible and a jug of water. At eight o'clock at night his bed, a table and chair were bought in. Until then he could only sit on the concrete floor and stare at the cream and green walls, or the trifling light which filtered in through the small barred window high in the wall. When he was tired of sitting he could stride around the high-walled narrow room, a human isolated in captivity. Once a day for an hour at noon he saw the sky and breathed fresh air, when he was taken out into the prison yard for exercise, and only then did he see his fellow prisoners who occupied the other punishment cells.

No talking was allowed, each prisoner walking alone, 20 yards from the next man. They could pass the odd word when they bunched up to go into the yard and when they came back in, but that was all. And the only other time for talking was at the weekly bath session, when the pouring water and steam would cover a brief conversation.

Every morning at 7.30, Roberts was allowed out of his cell to empty his chamber pot in the recess along the dark corridor, a relic of prisons built without in-cell sanitation. Then he was allowed to wash and given a razor blade so that he could shave under supervision, and return it to the prison officer on duty. His ablutions over, he had to carry his bed and the rest of the furniture into the corridor. His food was bread and water, the age-old prison diet for men on special punishment. Like most of the others, he refused to eat the dry bread and only sipped enough water to slake his thirst, as a protest against the sentence. When the special punishment finished he was brought the normal prison food.

In the cell next door was a friend of Roberts, whom I will simply call 'Carl' because he is now released and going straight. He and Roberts had been sentenced to 14 days solitary confinement for fighting with two other prisoners over the non-payment of gambling debt. Carl remembered vividly the misery of the period when he said: 'Ordinary prison life was bad enough, but it was bearable'. According to Carl there was work to do during the day, and because they had been in a few years they were allowed to associate with other prisoners in the evenings, playing darts, dominoes, or cards, and could read newspapers and books, listen to the radio and watch TV.

> The screws were reasonable, some because they were decent people, and some because no gaol which is under-staffed, as was Wormwood Scrubs, could run smoothly without the goodwill of the prisoners. And the food was tolerable. Everyone was always hungry and we could never get enough. But solitary was plain torture.

> The walls seemed to crowd in and the claustrophobia feeling grew worse by the hour in the uncanny silence which was broken only by the occasional measured tread of the patrolling officer, whose bunch of keys jangled as he passed the cell. It was almost a pleasure to hear him click back the cover of the "Judas" [inspection] hole in the door, and see his eye-ball through the tiny hole. Apart from exercise that was the only contact with another human being for the long stretches of the day.

He described how, one morning when he was exercising with Harry Roberts and were walking around the yard side-by-side. Roberts asked Carl how he was passing the time, and he told Roberts that he was going out of his mind, but also about some spiders he had been nurturing in his cell. Roberts begged him to give him one. The next day, the story continued, Carl took one of the spiders and carefully wrapped it in a piece of paper. When he went to the lavatory on the exercise yard, which was also used as a prisoner's post-box, he left it as they arranged, tucked behind the cistern. When they met going out to exercise the following morning, Roberts told him that the spider was installed and that he had managed to scrounge a small tin of condensed milk to feed it. For two days Roberts was a much happier man until the morning when an officer on patrol, known throughout the prison as a bully, opened the cell door. He found Roberts trying to feed his spider with a smear of condensed milk on his little finger. Roberts was so intent that he did not even look up.

The officer asked Roberts what he was doing and he replied that he was feeding his spider. With a derisive snort, the officer swept the spider to the floor and with his heavy boot crunched it to death. For a second Roberts was stunned, and then he fell on the officer, knocked him to the ground and got his hands in a stranglehold round the man's neck. Another officer, who was passing, came to the rescue and dragged Roberts away, and later he told Carl of the incident.

'He told me that Roberts looked completely mad … His eyes were bulging with hate and he was screaming'. Strangely enough the officer did not prefer any charges against Roberts, perhaps because he realised his action was certain to inspire a violent reaction in a man in close confinement.

In prison most of the younger men were keen on playing football or cricket, but Roberts had no interest and no talent for either game. On the rare days he was persuaded to play he would act the clown, falling down and pushing the other players off the ball, which amused the spectators but annoyed the players. He enjoyed being the centre of attention but disliked doing anything at which he could not shine. He wanted people to know about him. He wanted to have a reputation as one of the big men in the prison and, for that reason, he sometimes became involved in the battles of his friends. There was one time when one of his book-making friends had not been paid a gambling debt and the defaulting punter, when asked for the required amount of tobacco, made a point-blank refusal. It was known that this man had joined forces with the opposition bookmaking 'firm' and a full meeting was called of both sides and their supporters.

More than 40 prisoners met one evening and lined up, one side led by the debtor supported by his friends, and the other side by the book-maker with his backers. The bookmaker asked for his dues and the man again refused to pay. The honour of the prison bookmaker was at stake and there can be no backing away in such circumstances. Violence is the only accepted method of securing the future well-being of the aggrieved party in prison. He felled the debtor with a single blow, which would have been enough to satisfy honour; but it was not enough for Roberts, who fell upon the man, knife in his hand. The knife was pulled away before he could do any damage, but the incident gave Roberts a reputation for courage with some prisoners. Others were less charitable, suggesting he was merely trying to curry favour, joining in with a cause already won.

There was one time when he happily embarked on a quiet, danger-ous enterprise, which, on reflection, had its hilarious side. It was well known in the gaol that the officers had been awarded a pay rise which was retrospective and they were due several months' back pay. The news around the prison was that the money would be delivered on a certain Thursday and put into the safe, and that Friday would be the bonanza pay day. Two prisoners thought up the bright idea of stealing the money on the Thursday evening and they invited Roberts to join them.

The plan was to blow up the safe with gelignite obtained from one of the prisoners who was on an outside working party at Kew Gardens, where a number of big trees were being dynamited. He managed to steal some gelignite and detonators and on the Thursday evening Roberts, as a trusty, took two men from D-Wing to the cookhouse for cocoa. On the way they broke into the hut where the money was in the safe and, by the light of a torch they had brought with them, pushed the gelig-nite into its keyhole. They pushed in a detonator and wired it up to the electric light.

Then they took cover and one of them pressed the switch. Nothing happened. The same man turned off the switch and they examined the detonator, only to discover that it was the wrong type. Hastily they removed the gelignite, and were about to leave when they heard foot-steps. They took cover. In the darkness they waited, and heard the door open. One of them recalled, 'We thought it must be the screws and we were certain for at least another five years. A torch beam shone quickly around the room and then three men came in. They were carrying something heavy. The torch went on again and we could see three prisoners we all knew who had brought with them oxy-acetylene cylinders from the workshops with a special cutting tool. But they hadn't done their homework either, and no matter how hard they tried they could not get the apparatus going. After a couple of tries they gave up and we showed ourselves. It was the laugh of the century'.

'They took their stuff back to the workshop and we threw our gelignite and detonators over the wall. Then we went and got the cocoa on time and delivered it to the block. Nobody knew about it and none of the six of us ever talked. It was quite funny to see the officers after they had been paid out the next day. They were all pleased with themselves and Robbie and I laughed with our secret'.

Roberts had a considerable reputation as a storyteller, and while the more intelligent prisoners only half believed him, they were all prepared to listen. It was one way of passing the time and they listened to the long involved stories of the battles he had fought while serving in the Army. 'I thought he was a one man Army,' said one. 'Nobody else seemed to do anything. But we didn't mind too much because he told the stories so well and, anyway, we had nothing else to do'.

One story he told, which many of them believed, was demonstrably untrue. He said that the sentence of seven years he was serving was for keeping a brothel and that he had been forced to thrash a difficult customer which was why he was charged with inflicting grievous bodily harm. He also said that his wife betrayed him to the police, which was the one true part of the story. He was, undoubtedly, ashamed of his crime against the old man, and he knew with certainty that he would receive no sympathy for that. He told his listeners that he hated his wife and often gave her a beating, and his view was that all women should be thrashed frequently. His prison cronies also believed him about that, although he is only known to have struck his wife and his mother.

Another was about him among the prisoners at The Scrubs concerning an affair he had with a married woman while working on an outside working party. He kept this quiet for six months and his family say it only came to light when he went back to work inside and the woman wrote him impassioned love letters. Whilst Roberts was in prison for the robbery, he was the beneficiary of two changes to the criminal law that ensured leniency for those convicted of major crime.

Expansion of the Parole System

On Thursday 8 August 1963 at Bridego Railway Bridge, Ledburn near Mentmore in Buckinghamshire 15 robbers committed the Great Train Robbery. They stopped a train travelling from Glasgow to London with a travelling post office and got away with over £2.6 million (the equivalent of £51 million today), the bulk of which was never recovered. The majority of the robbers received sentences of 30 years imprisonment.

The length of the sentences provoked public outrage and the politicians who had proposed these sentences realised their mistake and expanded the system of parole under which prisoners became eligible to be released as soon as they completed half of their sentences. The result was that the deterrent effect of prison was lost. Roberts became a beneficiary of the new system and was released, only to kill three policemen.

Abolition of Capital Punishment

The abolition of the death penalty was brought about as a result of public opinion following the executions of two women, Ruth Ellis in 1955 and earlier in particular that of Edith Thompson in 1923, and partly miscarriages of justice in two major cases. The first was that of Timothy John Evans in 1950. Evans (20 November 1924 to 9 March 1950) was accused of murdering his wife and infant daughter at their residence at 10 Rillington Place in Notting Hill. In January 1950 he was tried and convicted of the murder of his daughter, and sentenced to death by hanging. During his trial, Evans had accused his downstairs neighbour, John Reginald Halliday Christie, of committing the murder. Three years after Evans's execution, Christie was found to be a serial killer who had murdered a number of other women in the same house, including his own wife.

Before his execution, Christie confessed to murdering Mrs Evans but not the baby. An official inquiry concluded in 1966 that Christie had also murdered Evans' daughter, and Evans was granted a posthumous pardon. The case generated much controversy and is acknowledged as a major miscarriage of justice.

The second was that of Craig and Bentley in 1953. On 2 November 1952, Derek Bentley (aged 19) and Christopher Craig (aged 16) burgled the warehouse of Barlow & Parker (confectioners) at 27-29 Tamworth Road, Croydon. Both men knew that Craig had armed himself with a Colt .455 calibre revolver and that Bentley was carrying a sheath knife and a spiked knuckle-duster. At around 9.15 pm, a nine-year-old girl in a house across the road spotted the two men climbing over the gate and onto to the roof of the warehouse. She alerted her mother who called the police. They arrived and arrested Bentley on the roof of the warehouse. He nevertheless shouted the ambiguous phrase, 'Let him have it, Chris' to Craig, who shot Police Constable Sidney Miles in the eye, murdering him. Eventually Craig was surrounded by police and, on running out of ammunition, he jumped off the ten metre high roof, breaking his leg.

At their trial at the Old Bailey, prosecution counsel claimed that the phrase, 'Let him have it, Chris' meant 'Shoot him, Chris', whilst defence counsel asserted that it meant, 'Give him the gun, Chris'. There was also disagreement over whether Bentley was fit to stand trial. A Dr Hill reported that Bentley was illiterate, of low intelligence, borderline retarded, and that he had been diagnosed to be suffering from epilepsy. English law at the time did not recognise the concept of diminished responsibility due to retarded development, though it existed in Scottish law (it was introduced to England by the Homicide Act 1957).

Eventually, both men were convicted of murder. Bentley was adjudged to be fit to plead and as an adult was sentenced to death by hanging. Craig, because he was a juvenile, was sentenced to be detained at Her Majesty's pleasure, and was released after ten years. Bentley was hanged less than three months after the burglary, having exhausted all his appeals. When the media pointed out that the man who had murdered the police officer had only been sent to prison, whilst a retarded adult who had hurt nobody had been hanged, there was a public outrage.

In 1965, the Murder (Abolition of Death Penalty) Act was passed by the House of Commons by 200 votes to 98 and by the House of Lords by 204 votes to 104. This suspended the death penalty in England, Wales and Scotland (but not in Northern Ireland) for murder for a period of five years, and substituted a mandatory sentence of life imprisonment. This meant that Roberts, Duddy and Witney would not receive the death penalty that they arguably deserved for murdering three detectives. It is ironic that the shooting of one police officer (Sidney Miles in Croydon) in the eye prompted the legislation that saved Roberts, Duddy and Witney from the death penalty for shooting another police officer in the eye (David Wombwell in Shepherd's Bush).

On leaving prison, Roberts immediately returned to his criminal activities, and quickly joined up with John Witney to carry out 'dozens' of armed robberies, concentrating on soft targets like rent collectors, bookmakers, post offices and the occasional bank. He later said, 'The most I earned was £1,000 from a single job. Witney was the eldest, the boss; he knew the best places to rob. Duddy joined us later'.

Roberts' time in the Army had given him a keen interest in firearms and he frequently discussed carrying and using them with his associates. His partnership with Witney was founded on a shared interest in them and Duddy also shared that interest. But even friends and associates of Roberts had their doubts about him. At one club, just off Regent Street, detectives found that Roberts had been an occasional visitor and that he drank with a man known only as Frank, who lived in south-east London. The man was found and eventually told the police that Roberts had asked him to take part in a big robbery near Bristol. He was able to tell them that he had been driven by Roberts down to the place where the raid was to be made and had been told that the prize would be worth many thousands of pounds. He confessed that he had been prepared to take part in the raid until he knew that Roberts was going to carry a loaded gun. It was at that point he withdrew from the scheme.

It was this lead to south-east London which led to inquiries being made in the Elephant and Castle area, and there it was found that Roberts had tried to get recruited to a gang who were planning a bullion raid. The reputation that he had built up around him in criminal circles had travelled sufficiently for the planners of the coup to be interested. He was invited down to a café in one of the backstreets — criminals mostly drink tea when planning a crime — then he began to show off. He told his prospective employers: 'I'll shoot anyone'. They showed him the door and dismissed him, in their words, as a 'nutcase'. The careful criminal does not use firearms and does not like those who do.

This, then, was part of the pattern of Harry Roberts, double killer, the man police wanted to find more than any other in their history. Slowly, the character of this man, who had never been important (except maybe in his military role), began to emerge as what might loosely be described as schizophrenic, at most times reasonably kind and gentle, but at others, uncontrollably and suddenly extremely violent.

CHAPTER 8

The Women in Harry Roberts' Life

The three women central to Roberts' life and already mentioned in *Chapter 5* refused to co-operate with the police enquiry into his activities. Whether this was due to his charm, considerable wit, charisma or just simple fear of a man who regularly relied on violence, and who had just murdered three policemen in cold blood, must be left to the reader to judge. This chapter pieces together what they told others (that they could have told the police) about the man at the centre of their inquiries.

As a boy, Roberts went to an all-male boarding school from the age of seven. On leaving school, he worked as a builder, before joining the British Army and was sent to Malaya and Kenya to deal with the uprisings in those countries. He returned to the UK, took-up a life of crime and was sentenced to several terms of imprisonment. He was 30-years-old when he murdered the three policemen and as a result lived in all-male gaols for close on the next 50 years, eventually being released at the age of 78. He has, therefore, had little contact with women during most of his life.

When imprisoned for robbery and assault on an old man, Roberts was detained at Wormwood Scrubs Prison, just a few yards from the scene of the Braybrook Street massacre. It is situated next to Hammersmith Hospital and its Nurses' Home in Du Cane Road. Prison Rules meant 'lights out' at 10.00 pm each and every night and many men found it difficult to get to sleep when they had been used to staying up after midnight on the outside. Looking-out of their cell windows, they could see lights in the Nurses' Home and soon realised that they could observe the nurses returning there, getting changed going to bed. Roberts, like many of the men took an interest in this nightly ritual and set up a communications system to alert fellow inmates to the best-looking nurses.

Following his arrest for the murders he spent a considerable time in solitary confinement, due to the threat that he posed, and he was kept under close observation by prison warders and one of the facts that they noted was that there was no evidence whatsoever of him masturbating whilst in prison. Men incarcerated for long periods usually feel the need to relieve themselves in this way, but not Roberts.

Mrs Dorothy Roberts: Harry's mother

Probably the most important and influential woman in Roberts' life was his mother, Harry had always been the apple of her eye and she worked hard to give him the best education and start in life. At the time of the murders she was 53-years-old and was living in a block of flats on an estate at the back of Euston Station, where she had been for over 20 years. Among things she told various were that Dorothy claimed that at the exact time of the shooting of the detectives a blackbird flew through her kitchen window and she had to call the caretaker to get rid of it for her. She felt that it was an omen of some kind.

Dorothy was an Irishwoman, with red hair and green eyes. She spoke softly with an educated English accent. She had worked exceptionally hard throughout her life to improve the situation for herself and her son. She frequently expressed her pride at having paid for everything that the family needed, and for refusing to accept handouts from the State. She was for example proud of paying for her son to be evacuated to Wales during the war and for him to go to college, so that 'he spoke beautifully and had beautiful handwriting'. She spoke proudly of a letter that 'My Robin' had sent her from Malaya, expressing his appreciation for the education that she had given him and the advantages that it gave him over his fellow soldiers.

She told reporters that Harry was born at 8 pm on Tuesday 21 July 1936 in the Maycroft Nursing Home, Woodford, which cost her 14 guineas a week (£14.70 pence or approximately £1,000 in today's money—a lot in those days). He was overdue, and he weighed eleven lbs, two oz. It was touch and go whether he would live or die.

Her husband, also called Harry, was in the Royal Air Force. He 'wasn't a nice man', always taking money off her and putting it on the dogs or drinking it away. He used to knock her about and she often thought he was 'mental'. His father committed suicide at the second attempt. His wife had left him because he was so violent to her. His grandfather ruined the family, who were well-to-do for the times, and was found dead in the snow, with his wife. They were by then reduced to selling matches and laces.

Dorothy separated from her husband whilst Harry was away at boarding school, St Joseph's Academy in Beulah Hill, and, as a consequence, she had to work even harder to keep him at the school and provide for him. Dorothy identified allowing him to become a day boy instead of a boarder when he was 13 as a bad decision. She explained how he pestered her to allow him to do so, and struggling as she was financially she found the proposal interesting as he could live at home cheaply and she enjoyed his company. Unfortunately, he immediately started truanting, pilfering from her purse and getting up to mischief. No amount of beatings from her made any difference.

When Roberts was identified as a suspect for the murders, and the police wanted to arrest him, her flat was one of the first places to be searched. The police went there in strength, as one might expect for the arrest of a man suspected of having cold-bloodedly murdered three policemen a few days earlier, for no apparent reason. They would have quietly surrounded the flat and satisfied themselves that they had covered all the entrances and exits so that nobody could enter or leave it, and then double-checked to ensure that they could deal with a man who was quite probably still armed and who could come out shooting. Only when the officer in charge was entirely satisfied that he could deal with any eventuality would they have knocked on the door and announced themselves.

It would only have taken the officers a couple of minutes to satisfy themselves that Roberts was not there and that he had not been so since the murders. The vast majority of the officers would have then withdrawn from the address whilst a couple of detectives questioned Dorothy about what she knew, whether she had heard from Harry since the murders and where she thought that he might go to hide. The officers would also have pointed out that Harry was suspected of killing three policemen and that he was probably still armed, and that the officers who would be searching for him would be concerned for their safety and carrying guns themselves. The potential for Harry to be shot and killed, either deliberately or by accident, was high. The sooner he was captured, the safer he would be. If she did know anything, it would be in his and her interests to tell them. Dorothy would have been seen as a prime source of information for the enquiry and any information that she gave would have saved a considerable amount of legwork for the police, so it is safe to presume that the interview was quite long and detailed. The officers would have wanted to ensure that Dorothy understood the danger that her son was facing with so many armed men searching for him, so that she co-operated fully with the enquiry in order to ensure his safety.

Eventually, however, her police interview was concluded and the detectives went back to Shepherds Bush Police Station to report their findings. Superintendent Chitty would have been impatiently awaiting their report so that he could decide his next move and report to the MPS Commissioner and Home Secretary, who would have been taking a keen interest

Two women police officers were left outside Dorothy's flat and, over the hours, days and weeks that followed, it was agreed that they could move into it with her. For the officers it meant that they were better able to see and hear what was going on and to keep warm and dry and get a cup of tea when they wanted one. For Dorothy it meant that she could show the police that she had nothing to hide and felt it would have seemed less obvious that she was being spied on. The policewomen who were in the flat for several weeks remembered a neat and tidy home with a bright hall, kitchen, bathroom and a sitting room carpeted in grey and with hand-embroidered antimacassars on the armchair. Dorothy served them tea in china cups while she recalled her life with her son and the ultimate tragedy which would take him to prison under a life sentence.

She appreciated the help that she received from the police and came to rely on them. 'I will say this for the police. They were good all the time. I had them billeted on me, for ages … they gave me no trouble. They used to bring their own tea, milk, and sugar and put shillings in the meter when they boiled a kettle. Sometimes they would even go and do a bit of shopping for me if I wasn't well'.

In the next few days, women police officers were posted to watch the homes of the other women in Roberts' life. A small squad of women officers was set-up and Det Insp Jack Slipper was put in charge. It was essential work to observe these women and ensure that Roberts' options in finding somewhere to live or hide were closed down, but he was never seen at any of the addresses, and as far as can be assessed never returned to the London area.

When the police first came looking for Harry, Dorothy claimed that her mind 'had gone blank' as the detectives told her about the murders and she started to wonder what had gone wrong and how she could have been a better mother and stopped it all. Although she christened her son Harry, Dorothy called him 'Robin', a name he had been given by a nanny when he was a toddler ('Harry had a nanny as a baby—it was she who nicknamed him Robin. He was a strong, healthy, intelligent boy, and affectionate ... I can only think he inherited his father's tough nature').

In the years that Harry spent in prison, she tried to understand what had gone wrong and how he had finished-up in so much trouble. Her thoughts always took her to a time when he was around 16 or 17-years-of-age and she had had a friend follow him to a man's flat. She had also gone to the flat and banged on the door. She found him there, 'all dressed up'. She formed the opinion that the man was a 'criminal-type' and that the two of them were up to no good. She made Robin go home with her. When they got there and closed the door, Robin turned on his mother, attacking her wildly. He punched her in the face, splitting her lip. She ran out of the flat, claiming to be going to the police station to report the assault, but could not bring herself to turn him in. After his conviction for murdering the policemen, she wondered whether it would have been better if she had done so, and whether he might then have turned out differently.

She said Robin wanted to be a police officer and hoped to join the CID. How could a young man who aspired to join the CID evolve into the greatest killer of CID officers in British history and in just a few years? Maybe he wanted to exercise power and authority over others, but lacked the personal discipline to accept discipline. Dorothy encouraged his interest in the law, but privately hoped that he would become a solicitor. Conversely, during her reflections on what had gone wrong for Robin, Dorothy identified that he had always done well under discipline, at boarding school, in the Army, and even in his first short visits to prison, at Wormwood Scrubs and in Maidstone Prison, where he had been made a trusty.

But she realised that when Robin deserted from the Army in Malaya things had started to go seriously downhill. She realised that something was badly wrong when he turned up on her doorstep before he was due to return from duty and she attempted to persuade him to go back and give himself up, but the Military Police came around first and picked him up.

She said he went out with a couple of 'nice women' and she had hoped that he might settle down, but these relationships soon broke down and he went back to his old ways. She told of how she always tried to be there for him. It broke her heart when the police told her that he had been arrested for coshing an old man, but she never missed a prison visit. When he left school, I arranged loads of interviews for him, but he never turned up for them. Then he did his four-and-a-half year stretch for robbing the old man and he swore that when he got out he would go straight. Dorothy took him to Camden Town and spent £100 on new clothes for him, so that he would not have an inferiority complex and could start looking for a job and a girlfriend, and get settled.

When he was on the run following the police murders, things got too much for her and she took an overdose and tried to commit suicide, but then called the police and they took a doctor to see her who saved her life.

'He was a very tidy boy. Spotlessly clean. That was college and Army training. Even when I saw him at Shepherds Bush when they caught him, and I walked past him at first because of his beard and long hair, he was clean. The police told me everything in his camp [in the woods] was spotless too. I cried when I saw him, and he hugged me. I asked him if the police had touched him and he said, "No, they have been the essence of kindliness". Even now he is prison, he says the same. Do you know, in a way, I am glad he is there—at least he can't get into trouble again. I asked him if he had seen me on television when I made my appeal, or heard me on the radio. But he hadn't. I told him I had tried to call him in for his own good. Colin Howard, husband of June, who saw me on television, told me he saw other people cry. He said I had gone over so well. I thought it was best to call Robin in for his own good'.

Dorothy received 'some terrible letters' when her son was on the run, telling her that if she paid certain sums they would tell her where her son's dead body was located; but also kind ones from strangers, enclosing money, which she gave to police funds. Convent educated in Ireland, all her life she tried to be respectable and work hard. She assured reporters, 'I've got to go on living for my son's sake. When everybody else has forgotten him, I will still be visiting him. But there doesn't seem to be much point in living now, and most nights I cry myself to sleep'.

Lilian Perry and June Howard

The police also visited two other women. One was Mrs Lilian Perry who, in recent years, had known Harry better than anyone else; the other was his old friend and sometime landlady, Mrs June Howard, who lived with her husband, Colin, and three children in a flat in Wymering Mansions, Maida Vale. Again, Mrs Perry always called him 'Robbie', and remembered him as the kindest man she ever knew saying that they never had a cross word the whole time they were together, that he hated rows, and would walk out of a room to avoid one although he told her he often rowed with his mother and used to walk out at home.

Lillian Perry described him as 'a quiet man, who kept himself to himself'. He hated pubs and clubs and just liked to sit at home and watch TV or read. Wrestling was his favourite programme and he read all the James Bond books. He was, she thought, 'a deeply lonely man' and wanted her to go everywhere with him; even if he just wanted to take his car to the garage to fill it up with petrol, she had to go with him. It seemed he couldn't bear to do anything alone. If he was working late on the building site she would take his tea over to him, and then he would insist on her staying until he had finished work. His reluctance to get involved in rows probably reflected the family rows that he experienced as a young man when his mother challenged his father about his drinking and his gambling. As he grew up, Roberts preferred to run away from rows, but when he was unable to do so that is when he resorted to violence, as when his mother confronted him when he was 16 or 17, for meeting an 'unsuitable' man in a flat.

Roberts' solitude also seems to have reflected his time at boarding school, in borstal, in the Army and in prison. He would have learned self-reliance and the ability to survive without human company. Lillian Perry described how, 'When he bought the big Daimler he would go and fetch his workmen in the morning and drive them over to the site. If they were hard-up he would give them money. He didn't believe in lending. He always seemed to be popular and was generous. I could have anything I wanted. He used to come home from work, throw his pay packet on the table and say, "Have what you want and save the rest". There was often more than £40 in the packet'.

When her daughter married he bought Mrs Perry a whole new outfit, everything from top to toe: a three-quarter length off-white swagger coat, turquoise silk dress, and matching shoes, hat, bag and gloves of real leather. Altogether he spent more than £30. He paid all the bills and would often 'give me a tenner' to give June. His only personal extravagance was his car, 'his idol and he would often take me on long drives and stop at the best hotels …'.

According to Mrs June Howard, Roberts worked hard to play a full part in family life. He took her children to hospital, the dog to the vet and even impersonated the children's father at their parent's evening, but he had his lazy side and often said 'If you can get plenty of money the easy way, why work for a little the hard way' which also seems to have been her philosophy. He had told Mrs Perry something similar, 'It was the Labour Government's fault'. According to Harry, if they hadn't put the squeeze on and killed the building trade, he wouldn't have ended-up inside. It was only when the trade flopped that he took to doing 'jobs'. He had told her that he would have to turn to crime and 'I didn't try to stop him because you can't order a man of 30 about'. But she had hoped he didn't really mean it, and thought if they never discussed it he would drop the idea.

Harry, she claimed, had to have money. He always had money as a boy. His mother had given him plenty, because she was working and could not spend much time with him. Harry later said it salved her conscience. So he could always buy friends with money but he could never rid himself, even as a boy, of loneliness. 'That's why he was happy with me, I think. There was no sex between us. I'm sexless and Robbie didn't like it either'.

June Howard knew him for more than ten years and she recalled that she had 'Only known him with two women, "that wife of his" and Lilian Perry. He had a funny puritan streak so that if her husband went "with birds", or asked Robbie to go to a club where there were women, or told dirty jokes, "or I undressed in front of him in the flat", he became shocked and even angry'.

Lillian Perry's experience was the same and seemingly he hated young girls, especially if they were 'all made up', or 'dressed sexy'. He was much younger than her, but she never felt it, because he was so quiet and homely. She suggested that he had never had a real home life before so that he loved getting home at night, seeing a big fire and finding a steak grilling for him. He used to say that was the life, and they would sit there peaceful and happy. She explained that she had never had that sort of kindness from her husband and that was why she stuck with Harry, and kept visiting him. She had worked out that he would probably only be 60 when he came out, and he was a good prisoner (actually he was much older, 78-years-old). He had always sworn to stay out of prison!

She told the press that on the day of the murders, 12 August 1966, she was expecting Roberts home with her by half-past-five but he didn't arrive until seven o'clock. She knew at once that something was wrong. He apparently looked as if he had been running, was breathless and flushed. She told him she had some nice rock salmon and chips for his tea but he looked disgusted and said, 'I can't eat anything... I'm sick up to here', and put his hand on his throat. She couldn't get him to eat anything at all. She said, 'Did you hear about the three policemen?' and he said, 'Shut up... It was us'. He told her they had been cruising round looking for a car to knock off to do a job. They couldn't find one, and he decided to pack it in and go home, when the police stopped them. Over-and-over again, he kept saying, 'If only that fool hadn't asked to look inside the car it wouldn't have happened. People have been warning us for over 12 months that if we were caught with guns we'd get 15 years. I kept thinking about that. I knew if the coppers turned the car over they'd find the guns and put us all away. I thought it was better to shoot it out than go down for 15 years'.

He kept staring at TV all the evening, but seemingly without seeing a single programme. He looked far away and when he turned to Lillian if she spoke to him, they were all misted over. He stayed flushed all evening, as if he had a fever. 'I went to bed when TV closed down … Harry said he would make himself up a bed on the put-you-up in the lounge. He kept on saying he wanted to burn the van'.

The following morning they went shopping for groceries and when they came back John Duddy arrived saying that he had slept with the guns under his bed. Roberts said he wished he had kept one. He said he would feel safer with one in his hand, although he never wanted to use one again. He took the guns from Duddy and hid them under the bed. In the afternoon they went for a walk in Paddington Recreation Ground. Duddy walked in front and Harry carried one of the children, to hide his face, talking only to the children. Roberts had insisted, 'as usual', on getting back to the flat in time to watch the wrestling on TV. They all returned and he kept on asking Duddy to go with him and get rid of the Vanguard. He said he was worried about the fingerprints all over it. But Duddy was too scared, saying he didn't want to go anywhere near the car. About eight o'clock in the evening he asked June Howard to go with him. She said she didn't want to, but he begged her, leaving Duddy to baby-sit and they went to Lambeth together, and looked at the car in the garage. They didn't go in, but looked through the wooden slats. The car was still there. Harry kept on saying he wished Duddy would help him get rid of it. When they got home he went on at Duddy again, but Duddy refused to have anything to do with the idea.

June Howard hardly slept a wink the night before for worry, and was covered in bumps on the skin which irritated her. Roberts said it was 'nerves'. On Sunday morning they set out to bury the three guns. They were gone for about two hours. When they came back Harry said no they had buried them, but for everybody's good he wouldn't say where.

Again he couldn't eat any dinner. In the afternoon, when June and Harry were looking after the children, he rang Mrs Howard and said she had to come back to take care of them as he had to go somewhere on 'urgent business' and 'get out of London and hide away'.

'We went to a café, and although I wasn't hungry I ordered a salad. I told Robbie to eat a solid meal. He ordered his favourite, steak and chips but, after a couple of mouthfuls, he pushed it away and said he felt too sick to eat. We went to the hotel, but Robbie talked very little. He was thinking and eating all the time. After he had booked in we went straight to our room. There were twin beds. Neither of us undressed. People who think we were lovers because we spent the night together must be crazy. No man with the worry Rob had on his mind could have wanted sex. Robbie just lay on top of his bed staring at the ceiling and smoking. I knew he was thinking and I didn't like to speak to him. We didn't sleep at all that night.'

Every now and again Robbie said, 'What a mess I've made of things. What a bloody mess. If only that fool hadn't wanted to inspect the car'. In the early hours of the morning he had said, 'I've got to get away, pet. If I can keep hidden, lie low for a while, the whole thing may blow over. Perhaps we'll be together again in a few months'. So they left the hotel about 9 am. He left his case in the left luggage office at Euston and went and bought camping equipment. Then they got a bus to Epping and he hardly spoke on the journey. When he got out, he said, 'This is as far as you go, love'. She cried like a baby and hugged him and he cried too. He took his money from his pocket — about six pounds — and gave her six shillings-and-sixpence, saying, 'That should be enough for your fare into town. Sorry to leave you short, but I reckon I'm going to need it more than you'.

She wanted to stay with him, but he wouldn't her. Later, he didn't hold it against her that she turned Queen's evidence (i.e. gave evidence for the prosecution against him), saying, 'There was nothing else you could do, pet, you had to do it'. She remained disgusted and amazed at what happened and was not sure who the governor was, Roberts or Duddy.

Before he fled the city, Roberts had read the newspapers which told a story that one man had been detained and that a car had been found, and he was pretty sure that it was Witney. He had always told Mrs Perry he was fond of 'Jack'.

He was in a terrible state and according to Lilian,

'He was frightened for himself then but he was upset on Jack's account as well. If only they hadn't had the guns. Robbie always swore they were only for use as frighteners. He kept on saying that it would never have happened if only the sergeant hadn't come back to ask for their licence and insurance. They wouldn't have shot them if they hadn't decided to search the van'.

But Mrs Howard is on record as saying that she had a different view about the guns: 'If they were only for frighteners, they wouldn't have been loaded, would they? I feel in a way it was my fault the whole thing happened. Over-and-over again, I told the boys they would get 15 years if they were caught with guns. That must have been on their minds when the coppers stopped them. It was panic. Sheer bloody stupid panic!'.

Panic or not, the deed was done. Three policemen were dead and Roberts was already saying that it was not the fault of him or his confederates, but that of the victims for having the temerity to do their job properly, to decide to search a suspect car. This twisted thinking seems to be a fixed part of this extraordinary criminal who seemed to be prepared to lay the responsibility for any act of his at the door of someone else. He does not appear to have ever expressed any regret for leading his three-man gang to triple murder on that day. He did not seem to have any feelings that by his violent act he had turned the happy wives of Fox and Wombwell into sad widows, orphaned their five children and numbed the life of the widowed mother of Det Sgt Head. I deal with whether or not his attitude has changed in the closing chapter.

CHAPTER 9

So Why Braybrook Street?

The crowded crime scene in Braybrook Street within
the police cordon as the investigation began

As a detective, I look at every aspect of a case, in order to better understand what happened, and why it happened. I try to understand the motives of all those involved in a crime, so that I can better understand the strengths and weaknesses of the case and the best places to look for further clues. In studying the case of Foxtrot One-One, there is one aspect that I have constantly struggled to understand and that is what Roberts, Witney and Duddy were doing in Braybrook Street that day. These guys were robbers, targeting small-time street bookmakers and taking their cash off them, but Braybrook Street was a very quiet street, lined by the semi-detached houses of the Old Oak Common Housing Estate on one side and the wastelands known as Wormwood Scrubs on the other.

A possible solution came to me after reading two books on the British Spy, George Blake, *The Springing of George Blake* by Sean Bourke and *Jeremy Hutcheson's Case Histories* by Thomas Grant. In his book, Bourke relates the efforts that he made to assist Blake to escape from Wormwood Scrubs Prison, whilst Thomas Grant explains the importance of the prosecution of Blake at the Old Bailey and the passions that it generated on all sides, and I started to wonder whether the gang were in Braybrook Street attempting to assist Blake to escape from prison. The more that I read, the more that this made sense and I have found little to reject the idea, so I will explain my theory and allow you to judge it for yourselves.

A Short History of Wormwood Scrubs Prison

At the start of the 19th-century, Wormwood Scrubs was one of the largest undeveloped areas of open land close to Central London. In 1812, the British Army had secured the right to exercise its horses on there but was not permitted to develop the land. When they were not using it they allowed the public to do so. As one would expect, a large open space close to the capital attracted a considerable number of proposals for development, but few have ever been approved. Between 1875 and 1890 Wormwood Scrubs Prison and Hammersmith Hospital were built on the edge of The Scrubs and, around 1930, the Old Oak Common Housing Association was formed and permitted to build houses on land bounded by Du Cane Road, Old Oak Common Lane and Braybrook Street.

Construction of the prison began in the winter of 1874, with the building of a small prison made of corrugated iron and a temporary shed to serve as a barracks for warders. Nine hand-picked prisoners, all within a year of their release, completed the buildings after which 50 more inmates were received. They in turn erected a second, temporary prison wing. Building then began on the permanent prison seen today, with bricks manufactured on site. By the summer of 1875,enough bricks had been amassed to build the prison's first block and its ground floor was finished as winter closed in. Construction was completed in 1891. In 2009 parts of the building were Grade II listed, principally because of its magnificent and distinctive gatehouse.

During World War II the prison was taken over by the War Department and the prisoners were evacuated. It was used as secure office space for the duration of hostilities and housed MI5 and MI8. Its many problems over the years include: IRA prisoners staging a rooftop protest; staff being accused and convicted of brutality; and being the subject of certain adverse reports by HM Chief Inspector of Prisons, and the Prisons Ombudsman (now Prisons and Probation Ombudsman) who also made recommendations to deal with suicide and self-harm. In 1982, the then Governor, John McCarthy, described it as 'a penal dustbin'.

At the time of writing, Wormwood Scrubs is a Category-B prison for adult males, whether convicted or on remand from the local courts many awaiting trial or sentence. Since April 2017, it has been operated by Her Majesty's Prison Prisons and Probation Service. It has an operational capacity (i.e. is officially allowed to accommodate) 1,279 inmates (2017) (see further and generally: www.justice.gov.uk/contacts/prison-finder/wormwood-scrubs).

A Road Alongside

In 1966, Braybrook Street was a pleasant, quiet, residential street, lined with long rows of 1930s terraced houses on one side and The Scrubs on the other. In those days, women still tended to stay at home and look after the house. There were fewer washing machines, tumble dryers, vacuum cleaners; the washing had to be done by hand and hung out in the garden to dry and brooms and carpet sweepers were often used rather than modern-day vacuum cleaners. This meant that the houses were 'being protected' and, because most of the women had children playing on The Scrubs, they were awake to any strangers in the area. The 20 foot high wall surrounding the prison meant that everybody entering or leaving did so through the main gate at the other side of the building.

So Braybrook Street 'went nowhere', had no buses, few cars and almost no pedestrians. The two large buildings in the area, the prison and the hospital were surrounded by high walls, with the entrances and exits on the other side of the buildings. There were women in the houses and young children playing football; there were no or few men in the area and any that were there would have come to notice.

Throughout the 1960s there had been a problem with prisoners escaping from British Prisons. The statistics for Wormwood Scrubs reveal:

1961	114
1962	Not published
1963	Not published
1964	93
1965	78
1966	86

With a 20 feet high wall around the prison and just one entrance and exit, it is not surprising that HM Prison Service focused its attention on the front gate and positioned its Security Department next to it. Most escapes therefore occurred over the wall at the back, near Braybrook Street.

Harry Roberts in Wormwood Scrubs

On 23 March 1959, Harry Roberts appeared at the Old Bailey, and was convicted of robbery and sentenced to seven years imprisonment, to run concurrently with another term of imprisonment that he was already serving at the time. He was sent to Wormwood Scrubs Prison, where he had kept himself aloof and avoided contact with other prisoners, but he had attended classes in French taken by another prisoner, George Blake. He had eventually been released at the end of his sentence early in 1966.

Roberts was therefore, familiar with the layout of the prison and its procedures, had contacts both among the staff and inmates, and perhaps most importantly of all, knew Blake himself. Following his release from prison, Roberts actively went around London searching for work. He went to Bethnal Green to meet the Kray Brothers and then to Camberwell to meet the Richardson Brothers, but they all felt that Roberts was too violent for them. Despite their reputations for violence and torture, London's premier gangsters preferred to secure co-operation with threats of violence, rather than dispensing actual violence. They were proud of restricting the real violence to members of their gangs rather than for the general public.

Partnering up with Witney and Duddy to bully street bookmakers into handing over the proceeds of their criminal activities, and who could not report the robbery to the police without being arrested for their own crimes, was small time for a man who, like Roberts was ambitious and perfectly happy to resort to serious violence. No doubt Roberts quietly felt that robbing bookmakers was merely a short-term activity to pay his bills until better remunerated employment became available.

There is little doubt that it was Roberts who brought the bag containing the three firearms that were used to kill the three detectives, but why would he do that? What did he have in mind? In their police interviews following their arrest for the murders the three men all claimed that they had planned to use the fatal day to find a new car, due to the poor condition of their current vehicle. They claimed to have spent the day driving around all the London Underground Stations in West London searching for a suitable vehicle to steal. But you don't need a gun to steal a car; it would simply increase the penalty for stealing the car.

John Witney and John Duddy

Witney considered himself to be the leader of the gang of robbers. The idea of robbing street bookmakers had been his, he had known the identities of the men concerned and their usual routes, and Witney had been working the scheme with other men before Roberts and Duddy. No doubt others had tried to take over the role of leader before Roberts, but probably few of them would have been as violent as Roberts. For the time being, Roberts appears to have been content to bide his time and let Witney run the show until Roberts was ready to make his bid for leadership. Duddy had no such ambitions. He was a small-time Glasgow villain, content to have a regular supply of income for the time being.

George Blake

Despite having an Egyptian Jewish father and a Dutch Protestant mother, and having been born and lived his life in Rotterdam, Blake was a naturalised British subject. In 1936 Blake's father died and he moved to Egypt to live with his father's family. When war was declared in 1939 Blake returned to Rotterdam, but was interned, escaping to England in 1943, where he was commissioned into the Royal Navy, subsequently being recruited into MI6, who sent him to Hamburg to take charge of the de-briefing of U-boat captains. When this was done he was then sent to the University for Cambridge to learn Russian in 1947 and 1948, before being sent to Seoul, Korea, to gather information on the Soviet Union, China and North Korea. When the Korean War broke out he was again interred. After a little more than four years he returned to England. Less than seven years later he was arrested as a Russian spy.

Blake was considered to be the most serious spy of the Cold War era, more important than Kim Philby, Donald Maclean, Guy Burgess and others. He had been employed on a number of most important operations and held senior rank. He was considered to have caused serious problems to both British intelligence and its allies, including the USA, and was generally considered to have been responsible for the deaths of 42 allied agents. There were calls at a very senior level for vengeance. He appeared at the Old Bailey in May 1961 before the Lord Chief Justice, Lord Parker of Waddington, charged with five offences under Section 1 Official Secrets Act 1911, for which the maximum penalty was 14 years' imprisonment. The Britain of 1961 was a different place to what it is today. The start of the liberal generation; the Beatles, hippies, Ban the Bomb, the Vietnam War, the rise of the IRA and of civil disobedience. Prison sentences were also much shorter than they are today. When, in 1964, the Great Train Robbers were sentenced to 30 years' imprisonment for what was dubbed 'The Crime of the Century' there was public outrage. There was real interest in what the Lord Chief Justice would impose on Blake.

It has been claimed that the judge contacted the Prime Minister for advice on the sentence that he should impose. Apparently, after some discussion it was decided that Blake should be awarded the longest determinate term of imprisonment in English legal history, a total of 42 years, being the maximum of 14 years on each of three of the cases, with two of the other terms being made concurrent (coincidentally making one year for each of the deaths of the people that he was alleged to have betrayed to the Russians). Those used to maximum sentences of 20 years (except for people convicted of murder or manslaughter who were sentenced to life imprisonment, but usually given parole some time after ten years) were outraged. Many spoke of assisting Blake to escape.

It was in September 1965, four years after his imprisonment and two years after the Great Train Robbery that Blake decided to make his first escape attempt, possibly prompted by the successful escapes of two of the Great Train Robbers, Charlie Wilson escaping from Winson Green (now called Birmingham) Prison on 12 July 1964 and Ronald Biggs from Wandsworth Prison in south London on 9 July 1965.

In *The Springing of George Blake* Sean Bourke relates how he (Bourke) was interviewed by the Hostel Board at Wormwood Scrubs in the first week of November 1964. The authorities decided that his conduct justified his being transferred to the hostel next to the prison at the end of the last week in November 1964 and he was then able to start to research the possibilities of assisting Blake to escape.

The following Monday, Bourke was allowed day release for the first time, and was hoping to arrange Blake's escape in December or January. As his plans developed, Bourke realised two things quite quickly. Firstly, that the best place to conduct any escape would be in Braybrook Street and, secondly, that he would need around £700 of working capital to make the plan work. He approached Blake's mother and sister, Adele, for the money. His plans were held up by their requirement that he first disclose the details of his plan. He was compelled to seek the funding elsewhere, which considerably delayed the escape.

At the beginning of June the police intercepted three Russians in London, a KGB active service unit sent to carry out Bourke's plan. They were detained and extradited. Then, ten weeks later on 12 August 1966 the detectives of Foxtrot One-One found Roberts, Witney and Duddy in Braybrook Street and were ruthlessly murdered. A further ten weeks passed before, on 22 October 1966, Blake escaped, assisted by Bourke and two friends. Is it possible that in June 1966 when the KGB active service unit was foiled, the Russians panicked and looked for a suitable gang of local criminals to affect the escape for them? Perhaps the Russians were less sensitive than the Krays and Richardsons and prepared to use Roberts and his pals and possibly even to arm them with pistols and revolvers. Then, when Roberts, Witney and Duddy were arrested, they decided that the best idea was to get a couple of Bourke's pals to do the job, and lend them the £700 that they needed to do it. Whilst there is no proof of the Russian link, and there never will be, there was clearly pressure to bring Blake 'home' to Russia and to further embarrass the British Government and MI6.

The day on which the detectives were murdered started with them delivering their boss, DI Coote to Marylebone Magistrates' Court with all the grappling irons, ropes and other bulky exhibits that he required to prosecute another case of escaping from Wormwood Scrubs. This may well have been on their minds when they saw the Standard Vanguard.

CHAPTER 10

The Trial

'I think it likely that no Home Secretary, given the enormity of your crimes, will ever think fit to show mercy by releasing you'.

Mr Justice Glyn-Jones addressing the gang in December 1966.

Because of the long hunt for Harry Roberts, both Witney and Duddy appeared at West London Magistrate's Court without him in September and were committed to stand their trial at the Old Bailey. On 14 November John Edward Witney, 36, slim and fair-haired, wearing a sports jacket over an open necked shirt, and John Duddy, 37, a burly man in a grey suit, were put into the dock of the famous Number One Court heavily guarded by prison officers. The indictment contained ten counts:

COUNT ONE: Against Duddy, aged 37, a driver of Treverton Tower, Treverton Street, North Kensington, W. and Witney, aged 36, unemployed, of Fernhead Road, Paddington, W, charged together with Harry Maurice Roberts, with murdering Detective Constable David Wombwell.

COUNT TWO: Against Witney—Well Knowing Roberts and Duddy had murdered Wombwell, he received, comforted, harboured, assisted and maintained Roberts and Duddy.

COUNT THREE: Against Duddy—Well knowing that Roberts and Witney had murdered Wombwell, he received, comforted, harboured, assisted and maintained Roberts and Witney.

COUNT FOUR: Against both Witney and Duddy—That they together with Roberts, murdered Detective Sergeant Christopher Head.

COUNT FIVE: Against Witney—Well knowing Roberts and Duddy had murdered Head, he received, comforted, harboured, assisted and maintained Roberts and Duddy.

COUNT SIX: Against Duddy—Well knowing Roberts and Witney had murdered Head, he received, comforted, harboured, assisted and maintained Roberts and Witney.

COUNT SEVEN: Against both Witney and Duddy—That together with Roberts they murdered Police Constable Geoffrey Fox.

COUNT EIGHT: Against Witney—That well knowing that Roberts and Duddy had murdered Fox, he received, comforted, harboured, assisted and maintained Roberts and Duddy.

COUNT NINE: Against both Duddy and Witney—That on 12 August with Roberts, they had with them firearms with intent to commit an indictable offence, or resist their arrest.

COUNT TEN: Against both Witney and Duddy—That they had with them in a public place firearms with ammunition suitable for use with the firearms without lawful authority or reasonable excuse.

Both Duddy and Witney pleaded not guilty to all charges.

Sir Elwyn Jones QC, the Attorney-General, opened the case for the Crown in front of Mr Justice Glyn-Jones and a jury of nine men and three women. Elwyn-Jones said,

'These two men in the dock murdered in cold blood three police officers who were going about their ordinary duty of protecting members of the public. The case for the Crown is this—that each of these two accused is guilty of these three murders. First, both knew loaded guns were being carried; second, they were each willing and ready to use them if necessary, either in the course of committing crimes that they were contemplating that day, or to escape if anyone tried to arrest them.'

He continued by saying that the evidence resulting from the 'four terrible minutes and of children who saw part of what took place' inevitably contained some discrepancies. But what he would describe appeared to be a true and accurate picture of what happened.

'Witney was the driver of the Vanguard and Roberts was beside him. Duddy was in the back. In the van were two loaded pistols, a Luger and a .38 automatic. I suggest there was at least one more gun.

When questioned by the police, Witney was seen to produce his driving licence and it might well be that the officers indicated their intention to search the vehicle. That would have meant the discovery of the guns.

Detective Sergeant Head appears to have walked around the back of the van. At that moment Roberts produced a Luger pistol and shot Detective Constable Wombwell from his side through the driver's window. Wombell fell dead in the road shot through the head.

Detective Sergeant Head started back towards the police car. Roberts got out of the van and fired at him. It appears that the first shot missed. Detective Sergeant Head saw Roberts and shouted, "No. No. No."

As he tried to take cover behind the front of the police car he was shot in the back and he fell dying in front of the police car.'

The Attorney-General went on:

'At that moment Duddy left the Vanguard armed with a .38 automatic. He ran to the nearside of the police car and fired through the rear nearside passenger window at Detective Fox. The shot shattered the glass.

It was not that shot, in the view of an expert, that killed Fox, because the bullet that did was found undamaged and not in the flattened condition in which it would have been had it gone through the glass panel.

Certainly, two more shots were fired from the .38 because afterwards three spent cartridges were found. The next two shots were probably fired through the open passenger window of the police car. One of them killed Fox. The bullet entered his left forehead, going out through the right temple.

The police car was a Triumph 2000 automatic. Police Constable Fox, would have kept the engine running and, as he was shot, his foot depressed the accelerator. The car moved forward, running over the body of Detective Sergeant Head.

Roberts and Duddy ran back to the Vanguard and Witney drove off, in reverse, as Witney did not like seeing the bodies lying in the roadway. The van disappeared down a turning.'

Sir Elwyn said the registration number of the Vanguard was taken by a Mr Deacon.

'The other thing known about the van of Witney's is that about 4 pm that afternoon it was driven into Witney's railway arch, 103. The evidence will be that it contained only its driver, who five minutes later walked away'.

Returning to the morning of 13 August, the Attorney-General explained that Mrs Perry would say Duddy joined Roberts at a flat belonging to a Mrs Howard and Roberts said, 'Oh God, what a mess we have made of things'. Duddy replied, 'I wish it had never happened'. Roberts said, 'We should have burnt the car because of the fingerprints on it'. 'On 15 August', Sir Elwyn went on, 'Witney after being told he was going to be charged with being concerned in the killings said, "I am worried about my wife's family. Will you give me five minutes to think things over and I may have something to tell you?" Witney said later, "I honestly did not shoot the coppers, guv'nor. I know you must have found out a lot and I will tell you the truth". Witney then wrote a statement'. Before reading it, Sir Elwyn said that evidence contained in it was evidence against Witney alone, not against Duddy. It began, 'As God is my judge, I had absolutely nothing to do with the shooting of any one of the three police officers, as no doubt witnesses can testify'. Witney said in the alleged statement that he had just driven into Braybrook Street when a small car pulled alongside and flagged him down. Two men got out, introduced themselves as police officers, and asked him whether it was his car. He replied, 'Yes'. One of them asked him if he had a road fund licence and he said, 'No'. 'One officer asked him for his licence while the elder of the two went to the side of the car,' the statement went on. 'Roberts leaned across and shot the young officer in the side of the face. The noise of the shot deafened and dazed me. The other officer ran towards his own car and Roberts leaped out of the side door, followed by Duddy, and gave chase, still shooting'.

The statement continued, 'I saw the second officer stumble and fall to the ground and Roberts fired again—I don't know how many times'.

> 'The third officer in the car tried to pull away but Duddy raced alongside and shot through the window of the car. They then raced back to the car, jumped in and said to me, "Drive."…I said, "You must be…potty." Roberts said, "Drive on…unless you want some of the same".'

'Witney,' the alleged statement went on, 'drove the car to Vauxhall'. Sir Elwyn said that on 17 August, Detective Chief Inspector Brown of Glasgow police, went to Stevenson Street, Glasgow, and arrested Duddy.

> 'On the way to Glasgow Central police station, Duddy said, "I was in the car but did not do the shooting. I would like to see my father because he is the only man I can talk to".

During the flight from Glasgow to London, Duddy told Detective Inspector Slipper, "Roberts started the shooting. He shot the two who got out of the car and told me to shoot. I just grabbed the gun, ran to the police

car and shot the driver through the window. I must have been mad. I wish
you could hang me now".'

Sir Elwyn said that later at Shepherd's Bush Police Station, Detective
Superintendent Chitty was told by Duddy that Roberts shot the man
who was talking to Witney, then turned and shot the other. 'He ran
towards the police car and Roberts got out and shot him in the back. He
stumbled against the car and fell to the ground. I got out – fell out — of
the car, and grabbed a gun. Somebody said to shoot him and I went to
the side of the car and shot the driver. He was trying to reverse his car
at us'. Duddy then said they all got back into the car and drove to the
garage at Vauxhall. Witney had arranged a garage 'to put the stolen cars
in. We were looking for a car and we were going to sit on the grass and
fix up to do a rent collector'.

The Attorney-General read a statement which he said had been made
by Duddy. It concluded, 'I didn't mean to kill him. I wanted quick money
the easy way. I am a fool'. Duddy had said to Detective Sergeant Berry,
'One thing I have appreciated is the way you have treated me. I had
expected rough treatment, especially after what I had done to your mates'.

A girl aged 14 told the court that her attention was drawn to a police
car in the middle of Braybrook Street and a van behind it. There were
three people in the van. Asked if any of the persons in the van resembled anyone, the girl replied, 'The driver resembled Bobby Charlton,
the footballer.

> 'Two of the three people in the police car got out and went back to the van.
> One seemed to be looking at the driving licence of the driver. The other
> walked round the van ....The policeman who was standing by the door
> started to walk back to the police car. The driver of the van and the front
> seat passenger got out with guns.'

The girl was shown a grey suit and said it was similar to the one she had
seen the man wearing. Counsel told the judge, 'Evidence will be given
later that this was the one that Roberts was wearing'. She said that she
saw the two men with guns in their hands. She gave a demonstration of

the size of the guns with her hands and agreed they were something like eight or nine inches long. Asked what was the first thing that happened after the two men got out and the policemen had gone back towards the police car, the girl said, 'A shot was fired and he slumped to the floor'.

She said she could not say which of the two men who got out of the van fired the shot. Asked what had happened to the other policeman who had been at the back of the van she said, 'He rushed forward as if to take the gun'. The policeman did not get further than the van before he was shot. She could not say which of the men shot the second policeman, who fell down by the van. Questioned as to what happened next to the two men who had got out of the van, she said, 'The driver got into the car and the other man ran towards the police car, the one who looks like Bobby Charlton. He was the man who had got out of the car on the driver's side'. She said the third man never got out of the van. The one who went to the police car fired a shot and the driver of the police car fell in his seat. She did not see anyone else fire any shots. She thought more than one shot was fired.

On the Sunday she went to a police station and was taken into a room where there was a man whom she recognised as the driver 'that looked like Bobby Charlton'. Asked if she saw him in court, she pointed to Witney.

A boy aged ten said he was in Braybrook Street when he saw a car stop. 'At first I thought it was acting,' he said. John Mathew, for the prosecution, asked, 'You thought a film was being made or something?' The boy replied, 'Yes, sir'. The boy said that he saw a van near the car. A policeman got out of the car and started walking over to the van. 'A bloke got out of the van and started shooting'.

'The policeman started running back to the car shouting, "No. No. No." A chap in a blue suit who got out of the van shouted, "Come on". And a man in a white jacket got out of the van and they both started shooting at the police car'.

Asked how many shots he thought were fired at the police car, the boy said eight or nine. Cross-examined by Hudson, the boy said that neither of the policemen had stood by the driver's seat of the van. Replying to

Comyn, the boy said he saw only two men in the van — one in a blue suit, the other in a white jacket. Both were carrying pistols.

There was an expectant air about the court the next day for both police and press knew that there was a strong chance of Roberts' capture, but it was not until after the luncheon adjournment that the Attorney-General rose from his seat and said to the judge, 'I think it is right I should inform Your Lordship that there is confirmation of information that the man Roberts has been arrested today. In the circumstances I would respectfully request your Lordship to adjourn this case until tomorrow morning so that the fullest consideration can be given to the situation which has now arisen'. James Comyn QC, defending Duddy, and W M Hudson, defending Witney, agreed and the judge told the jury, 'It seems I can give you the afternoon off'.

The next morning the court was crowded from the earliest possible moment. Everyone wanted to see the man who had been on the run for so long and who, it was alleged, had shot two of the policemen. They heard Leslie Boyd, the clerk of the court, say quietly, 'Put up Harry Maurice Roberts'. Every eye was on the oblong dock in the centre of the courtroom as two prison officers walked up the steps from the cells below, followed closely by the slight figure of Roberts wearing an open necked shirt, blue jeans and gumboots. His face was slightly sunburnt, but to the detectives and pressmen, who have great experience of seeing prisoners in the dock, Roberts seemed relieved, as if the burden of being so alone had been lifted, even surrounded as he was by the awesome panoply of a court which could have contained few people who did not feel acute revulsion at his savage crime.

Mr Justice Glyn-Jones then said, 'Well, Harry Maurice Roberts, a bill [of indictment] has been signed against you providing for your trial in this court together with two other men, Witney and Duddy, and that means the proceedings in the magistrate's court will be brought to an end and you will be tried together'.

Whenever a person is accused of a serious crime and is to be tried on an indictment before the Crown Court the case is almost always committed by the magistrates for a trial by jury. There is, however, an alternative route which allows a High Court judge to take control of the case and accelerate its path to the higher court. He or she directs the magistrates to discontinue their proceedings and the Crown Court to instigate proceedings against the accused. This means that the case is 'rushed' and that certain normal safeguards and procedures are not carried out, so the High Court judge should only rarely use the procedure and then only when satisfied that the it is in the interests of justice and does not unduly disadvantage the accused. Mr Justice Glyn-Jones was referring to the appearance of Roberts at West London Magistrate's Court, when he had been formally remanded in custody after a brief appearance.

Roberts' only words during the four minute proceedings were, 'Yes, please, sir' when asked if he wanted legal aid. The judge granted it and said that he proposed to set December 5 as the date of the trial. Sir Elwyn Jones, the Attorney-General, said he had no objection and Kenneth Richardson, who appeared for Roberts on that day, said the date was acceptable, and added, 'Only if it proves unavoidable will any application for an extension be made'. The judge agreed that applications could be made to him, 'But I shall want a great deal of persuading if any more time is needed', he warned.

Eight minutes after the court proceedings concluded, Roberts was driven in a car from the Old Bailey to prison. His head was covered with a blanket and he was handcuffed to a warder. Three weeks later, on December 6, the trial finally opened again. This time all three men were arraigned before the Old Bailey. Duddy and Witney pleaded 'not guilty' to the whole indictment. Roberts pleaded 'guilty' to murdering Detective Sergeant Head and Detective Constable Wombwell, but 'not guilty' to murdering Police Constable Fox. He also pleaded 'guilty' to being an accessory to the murder of PC Fox and 'guilty' to possessing a firearm in a public place.

This time the Crown was represented by the Solicitor-General, Sir Dingle Foot QC. As soon as the charges had been put, Mr Justice Glyn-Jones asked him: 'Do you accept the pleas of Roberts?' Sir Dingle said, 'No'. The judge said, 'Then I need say no more'. The trial then proceeded on the charges to which all the three accused had pleaded 'not guilty'.

Sir Dingle Foot opened by saying that when Roberts was arrested by a police sergeant in a barn in Sawbridgeworth, Hertfordshire, 13 weeks after the shooting on August 12, he had by his side a Luger pistol. Continuing his opening statement he said that on September 7, Witney said to Det Sgt Berry, 'How are the wives of the policemen who got killed? I cannot bear to think about the kids they had. Roberts and Duddy must have been mad'. On September 23, Duddy said to the same officer, 'You have got the impression that Witney was forced to drive back after the shooting. You can take it from me that Witney was the brains of this outfit'.

Sir Dingle said that on August 15, Roberts bought camping equipment and went with Mrs Lillian Perry by Green Line bus to Epping. There he left her, and he then apparently hid himself in Thorley Wood near Sawbridgeworth, Hertfordshire, and it was there that his tent was found.

On 15 November, Police Sergeant Smith started to search a Dutch barn about three quarters of a mile from the tent. Inside, Roberts was found in a sleeping bag hidden among some straw and he had a Luger pistol behind him. Lillian Perry said that Roberts had been living at her address in Bristol and she had been to London with him on occasions. In June she and Roberts came to London in his Daimler and they stayed at the flat of Mrs Howard at Wymering Mansions, Paddington. At different times she had seen all three defendants with guns.

On August 12, Roberts returned to Wymering Mansions at 7 pm. He seemed upset and said he had a terrible headache. That afternoon she had heard a news flash on the radio about the shooting of the policemen. She went on, 'When he came in I asked him if he knew anything about it, and he said, "Yes, it was us"'. When he went to bed he told Mrs Perry what had happened. He said they were in Braybrook Street when a police car came up. The policemen asked to see Witney's licence and he said it was slightly overdue. The police were not satisfied and wanted to search the car. Roberts then told her, 'That's when the shooting started'.

Mr Justice Glyn-Jones asked, 'Did he say what would have happened if they had searched the car?'

Mrs Perry replied, 'He said if the police had found the guns they would have done time for nothing because they were not out to do anything'. She said they spent Saturday night [August 13] at Wymering Mansions when Roberts kept the guns under his mattress. They spent the Sunday night at the Russell Hotel. On Monday [August 15], after Roberts had bought some camping equipment, she went with him by Green Line bus to Epping. There Roberts said, 'This is as far as we go together. I am on my own now'.

On the same day, doubtless unknown to Roberts, the man who was claiming the reward for the capture of the gunman, 21-year-old farmhand John Cunningham, made a three minute appearance in court at Harlow, Essex. Cunningham, who lived at Thorley Hall, Bishops Stortford, only a few hundred yards from where Roberts was captured, was accused of breaking into the factory at Sheering, Essex, of Walter Lawrence (Sawbridgeworth) Ltd, on November 11, and stealing £10 10s. That was three days before Roberts was arrested. On the day Cunningham was arrested, at 7.30 am November 11, he was charged and then released on bail. While the case was pending, Harry Roberts admitted responsibility for the theft. Application was made for the proceedings against Cunningham to be withdrawn and the Director of Public Prosecutions let it be known that he had no objection. It was not known at the Old Bailey that this little case was going on in Essex and that Roberts had told the truth so that an innocent man had not remained in danger of conviction. It was understandable, for at the court at which Roberts was the centre of interest, the drama was high.

When the preliminary witnesses had been dealt with the prosecution progressed to proving that the three men in the dock had their guns by firm intention, and for some long time. Mrs June Howard, told the court of money sent to her by her old friend, Roberts, to buy him a gun. 'He asked me many times to get him a .38,' she said. 'I said I would try to help. I kept on bluffing him into thinking I could get him a gun because I needed the money. I spent the £65 he sent me for a gun on the rent that was owing. But,' said Mrs Howard, at whose flat Roberts was lodging with his 43-year-old friend Mrs Lillian Perry when he shot the two policemen, 'I never supplied him with a gun, nor returned the money'.

Mrs Howard said Roberts' buy-me-a-gun requests were made when he was living in Bristol two years previously with Mrs Perry. They used to visit her in London. She had known Roberts for ten years, but it was not until the end of last year, or early this year, that she knew he had obtained a gun, she said. He threw a small canvas bag at her, told her to catch it and said it contained a gun. 'I asked him to take it out of the flat as the flat I was then living in didn't belong to me,' she said. 'Roberts said the gun could be used to frighten people who owed my husband money'.

In June and July of 1966, said Mrs Howard, she also met John Duddy and John Edward Witney at her flat with Roberts. Once, when Roberts and Witney were in the kitchen, Witney said, 'If we have them down we must be prepared to use them'. 'I guessed,' said Mrs Howard, 'that they were talking about guns'

On another occasion she was out with Roberts and Witney in Roberts' Daimler car. From the rear seat, Witney asked her, 'Would you pass me my right hand. It's in the glove compartment'. Mrs Howard said in a whisper, 'I opened it and found two guns. I didn't want to handle them at all. But Witney said, "Don't be silly, it's only small"'.

'I passed him the smaller gun. Roberts took the other and tucked it into his waistband. I was afraid the guns might be loaded. I had no way of telling'. She added that they then met Duddy and went to a public house together for drinks. She said she saw ammunition in her flat in June. There were bullets in a tin and in a jacket pocket. 'I told Roberts' she added, 'that I didn't like having them in my place'.

James Comyn QC, for Duddy, asked, 'When Roberts asked you if you could get him guns, didn't you ask him why he wanted them?'

Mrs Howard replied, 'No, I shouldn't imagine he would have told me if I had asked'.

Comyn asked, 'Did you suspect it was for criminal purposes?' Mrs Howard paused, twisted her hands on the ledge of the witness box, and whispered, 'I suppose so'. Comyn asked, 'As Roberts was not working when he and Mrs Perry were staying with you, did you suspect that he was living on crime?' Mrs Howard replied, 'There was no reason to suspect. He never seemed to have any money'.

'Did you know he was keeping guns in your flat?'

'No'.

Mr W M Hudson, for Witney, questioned Mrs Howard about drugs and Post Office Savings Bank forgeries.

'The day on which you were to give evidence three weeks ago you were taken to hospital with an overdose of drugs', he said.

Mrs Howard snapped, 'Not with an overdose. I was taking pethidine for rheumatic pains'.

'You were taking a good many at a time?'

'I was taking a tablet every four hours'.

'Is it right,' Hudson asked, 'that you have been questioned by the police about forging documents and getting money from the Post Office on them'. Mrs Howard agreed. 'In fact,' continued Hudson, 'you have admitted to the police that you forged a signature. You did that in the presence of all three defendants?' Mrs Howard nodded and said, 'Yes, knowing that two of them were carrying guns. I didn't quite know what might happen to me if I didn't agree to [it]'.

She said it happened after the incident of the two guns in the glove compartment of Roberts' car. 'They showed me a Post Office book and some withdrawal slips,' she explained. 'They asked me to forge the signature to make a daily £10 withdrawal. They wanted me to go to the Post Office and draw the money out. 'I agreed because I was afraid. I was frightened of what they might do to me as they were carrying guns. I didn't want to take any chance'.

Det Ch Insp Hensley said that on August 17, he was flying back from Glasgow with Duddy and Det Insp Slipper. Slipper said that Duddy made a statement beginning: 'It was Roberts who started the shooting'. He immediately wrote this in his book.

Comyn said, 'Duddy's instructions to me are that no statement was made on the aircraft, do you understand?'

Slipper said, 'I understand'.

Just as Slipper was about to leave the witness box, Comyn said he had just been handed a copy of the *Sun* newspaper, which contained a photograph taken from inside the aeroplane. The newspaper was handed to Slipper, who said that it showed him with Det Ch Insp Hensley and Duddy with a hood over his head. Duddy was still sitting in a chair, before he was allowed to sit on the floor. The newspaper was then handed to the judge and afterwards to the jury.

The trail was adjourned, and on the following day the defence opened.

Mr O'Brien, of Grange Road, Small Heath, Birmingham was called to the witness box and said that a year ago he and Witney were working at the same firm in Acton. They often used to go to *Tom's Bar Café* in Horn Lane, nearby. 'We were talking once about being in trouble with the police and how far you would go to keep out of trouble,' he said. 'Witney said life was his freedom. I told him I would not kill to get away'.

O'Brien said that four days before the Shepherd's Bush shootings he had sold Witney his own driving licence for £6. On August 15, he went to the police and told them about that transaction. That licence was found on Roberts when he was arrested. The prosecution was building up a formidable case, which proved how well the police, under the direction of Det Supt Richard Chitty, had done their job and marshalled their evidence.

Only one of the prisoners chose to give evidence, and that was Witney. In the witness box he appeared a quite intelligent man, well in command of himself. He was the only one really fighting because he had not used a gun on the day of the murders. He said that early in June he bought for £20 a Standard Vanguard estate car. It was not taxed and the insurance cover ran out at midday on August 12. It was noisy and the reason it was untaxed was because it would not pass the Ministry of Transport (MOT) test. A few days before the shooting he had ordered a set of car number plates. It was intended that they should be fitted to a car he intended to steal. W M Hudson, for the defence, asked Witney, 'What did you intend to do with the stolen car?'

'Nothing particularly. Probably it would have been sold'.

'Was anyone going to help you?'

'I would have stolen the car myself. The two gentlemen in the dock might have helped me to change the plates and perhaps to dispose of the car'. Witney said he also rented a garage under some arches in Kennington. This was needed to house the car after it had been stolen.

On Friday August 12, Witney said, he left home just before 8 am and drove to Duddy's flat. He had arranged to meet Duddy and Roberts there. 'We were going to look out for a car to steal,' he said. Roberts was carrying a shopping bag in which was a pair of dungarees. Hudson asked, 'Had you the slightest idea that underneath those overalls were firearms?'

'I had not the slightest idea'.

'Did the use of firearms come within your contemplation?'

'No. It would be utterly ridiculous. If you are caught the maximum you are likely to get for taking and driving away is six months'.

Witney said that he, Roberts and Duddy visited a number of railway station car parks looking for a suitable vehicle to steal, but they did not find what they had in mind. 'We arrived at East Acton station at about 3.15 pm. There we decided to give up the venture for the day,' Witney told the jury. 'I could not go home because my wife thought I was at work'.

Hudson said, 'I want you to tell us, slowly and clearly, what happened after you got into Braybrook Street, Shepherd's Bush'.

Witney said, 'I had gone approximately 20 to 25 yards when the police car drew up alongside. I was driving. Roberts was next to me and Duddy was in the back. The bag containing the guns had been put between the front and rear seats. As the police car pulled alongside, Sergeant Head flagged his hand.

'I stopped and parked close to the kerb. Sergeant Head and Detective Wombwell got out and came towards my window. Sergeant Head asked me for my road fund licence and I explained that I didn't have one. He asked me why and I said I could not get it taxed until I got an MOT certificate. Then he asked me for my driving licence and I produced it. Finally he asked me for my insurance certificate and on reading it he remarked, "It is three hours out of date"'.

'Wombwell started to write down my name and address and I said to him, 'Can't you give me a break? I have just been nicked for this a fortnight ago'. And then the shot came. I heard no conversation between the officer and Roberts. The shot came from my left, but I didn't see the impact of the bullet. Wombwell had disappeared and Roberts jumped out of the car. I don't know whether he had fired the shot out of the window or not.

'I was pretty shaken. I opened my door and saw Wombwell lying on the road. By the time I had realised what had happened Roberts was going up the road after Sergeant Head. I heard the pistol being fired and I saw the officer fall to the ground. 'Duddy got out almost immediately after Roberts. Duddy ran alongside the nearside of the police car and fired through the window'.

Witney explained that both Roberts and Duddy ran back to the Vanguard. 'As Roberts got back into the front seat, he said, "Drive!" I said to him, "You must be... potty." His reply was "Drive!... unless you want some of the same." I reversed because I could not stomach driving past the policemen. My mind was in such a state I did not realise where I was driving'. Witney said later he and Roberts went to a café at Euston. 'Roberts said to me, "You look as though you are going to keel over." I was shaking like a leaf, sweating buckets. I could only drink half my cup of tea. Then we got a cab to Duddy's place'.

Hudson asked, 'Have you ever carried a firearm?'

Witney replied, 'Never, in any circumstances, except during my Army training'.

'What picture did you have of Roberts after this terrible thing?'

'He was a different person to the one I had known'.

'Had you ever seen him like that before?'

'No, never'.

'What was your attitude to him after this happened?'

'I was petrified'.

Witney said that he drove back to the garage in Tinworth Street and on the way Roberts was holding a gun in his hand. After garaging the car, he locked the door and gave the key to Roberts. Later that day Roberts asked him, 'You would not grass us, would you?'

'I said, "No", and he said, "Don't make that mistake. You know what happened to Jack Spot and his wife, and that was minor in comparison"'.

The judge asked, 'In comparison with what was going to happen to you?'

'That is what I took it to mean'.

Under cross-examination, Witney maintained that he was 'terrorised' by Roberts. He described as nonsense a statement by Duddy, which claimed that he [Witney] was 'the brains' behind the shooting.

James Comyn QC, for Duddy, in his closing speech said that the accused people presented a dirty picture, not of gangsters, but of petty, almost pathetic, criminals. 'Is it not the real truth,' he asked, 'that Harry Roberts carried guns because it made him feel bigger than the petty criminals he and the others were?'

'Neither in conscience nor in fairness can you find my client guilty of murdering Sergeant Head and Detective Wombwell. Roberts shot the officer standing at the car window as he was taking Witney's particulars. He went on in the most callous cold blood to shoot the second officer in the back, as he was running to safety. He was the man who started it all'.

There was not much to say for Roberts. James Burge QC, who had taken over his defence, tried by saying that it was clear that his client did not shoot PC Fox, although he admitted he was a prime mover in what happened and that he fired the first and second shots, but before the jury could find him guilty of that murder they must be satisfied there was a common purpose between the defendants to use guns.

Hudson, for Witney, said that the condition of Witney's car without a road fund licence and with a defective silencer, tied up with string, made it an open invitation for the police to stop him. 'In view of the car's condition, do you believe Witney was party to an enterprise involving the carrying of loaded firearms? He was only out to steal a car, an easy offence to commit these days'.

In his final speech for the Crown, Sir Dingle Foot said that no-one had suggested that the shooting of the police officers was anything but murder. That being so there were only three issues for the jury to consider: Who did the shooting? Did the accused have the common purpose of using guns in order to avoid or resist arrest? And if Witney was not a party to a common design was he an accessory after the fact in the sense that he helped the others to escape? At this point the trial was adjourned for the weekend; time for the police to relax after they had given evidence, and for the three accused to ponder their fate. On the Monday, when the judge finished his summing-up, it took the jury just 30 minutes to announce a guilty verdict against the three men for the murder of each of the three policemen. All three were found guilty of carrying firearms with intent to commit an indictable offence or resist arrest. The judge discharged the jury from giving a verdict on cross-charges that each harboured the others after the murders.

Passing sentence, Mr Justice Glyn-Jones said, 'I pass upon you the sentence prescribed by law for the crime of murder, on each count of which you have been convicted, that is imprisonment for life. You have been justly convicted of what is perhaps the most heinous crime to have been committed in this country for a generation or more'.

> 'I think it likely that no Home Secretary, regarding the enormity of your crime, will ever think fit to show mercy by releasing you on licence…This is one of those cases in which the sentence of imprisonment for life may well be treated as meaning exactly what it says…Lest any Home Secretary in the future should be minded to consider your release on licence, I have to make a recommendation…that you should not be released on licence, any of the three of you, for a period of 30 years, to begin from today's date'.

When, three years earlier, the Great Train Robbers had been convicted at Aylesbury Assizes of robbing the staff of a travelling post office of £2.6 million, in a crime that was referred to by the trial judge as the crime of the century, there was public outrage at the severity of the sentences they received. On this day, the only outrage seems to have been that these three defendants were not to be hanged. A petition for the re-introduction of the death penalty was immediately prepared and submitted to the Home Secretary for his consideration.

The Appeals

On 31 May 1967 the appeals of Roberts and Witney against both conviction and sentence were listed for hearing at the Court of Criminal Appeal. Neither prisoner was permitted to attend; this is not unusual as the cases are paper-based, with no witnesses being called or heard, although barristers are usually required to attend in order to briefly introduce their cases and to respond to any issues raised by the judges, based on an initial reading of the correspondence in the case. It is interesting to note that Duddy did not appeal. Often the reason for not doing so is a fear that the sentence will be increased (which is unlikely when it is the then second longest in modern criminal history!).

CHAPTER 11

Imprisonment For Life (Prisoner 231191)

On 12 December 1966, Harry Roberts was taken 'down the steps' at the Old Bailey. 'The steps' in question lead from the various docks in which prisoners sit during their trials, to the cells beneath the court. Standing at the counter with his two co-defendants, Duddy and Witney, waiting to be inducted into prison, there can be no doubt that Roberts had the sentence of life imprisonment and the recommendation that they all serve at least 30 years, ringing in his ears. Few people can imagine what that feels like.

This was at the time the second longest tariff ever handed down by a British court and reflects the judge's comments that this was 'the most heinous crime to have been committed in this country for a generation or more'. Only George Blake, the Russian spy had ever been sentenced to a longer term, although the Great Train Robbers, less than three years earlier, had received the same sentence. Roberts was 30 years-of-age at this time and, with an average life expectancy of 'three score years and ten', if he was released as soon as he had completed his time, he could hope for around ten years of freedom at the end of his life, as his health deteriorated. His prospects were not good.

These thoughts would have been rattling around in Roberts' head as he was presented to the principal officer in charge of HM Prison Service staff in the cells. He would have stood before this man to be informed of his earliest possible release date, to be searched and have his property listed, and to have his next of kin and their contact details recorded. The PO would then have reviewed the facts of the case, and what was known about the prisoner standing in front of him, and decided to recommend to the prison Governor that Roberts should be a Category-A prisoner.

Category-A prisoners are those seen as likely to attempt to escape, or to receive assistance from outside the prison in order to escape, or to be a particular risk to the prison community of prison officers and prisoners. They must be accompanied by two officers wherever they go, are not permitted to mix with other prisoners, and the Governor must be able to immediately inform the Home Secretary (nowadays the Justice Secretary) of their whereabouts at any time of the day or night, without receiving any assistance. Roberts would then have been taken to the cells to hear the most terrible sound in the world, a heavy cell door clanging shut behind him, to be left with his thoughts.

If Roberts had been a 'glass half-full type of guy', at this stage he may have remembered that it had only been eight months before he murdered the three police officers that the Murder (Abolition of Death Penalty) Act 1965 suspended the death penalty. He had narrowly evaded the hangman and his conviction prompted calls for the death penalty to be reintroduced and for all police officers in England and Wales to be routinely armed.

Roberts is a tough guy. He had been trained by British Special Forces to be a survival specialist in Malaya during the conflict. But to be told that your life is just about over and that you will be spending most, if not all of what is left to you, in a six feet by eight feet cell and slopping-out every day, it must be difficult to come to terms with. When you have a reputation for liking the ladies, knowing that you will be living in an entirely male community cannot be good news either.

A life sentence in England and Wales (and at that time) generally meant a very minimum of six years in prison, followed by a hearing before the Parole Board and possibly an early release under Probation Service supervision to ensure that the prisoner did not return to a criminal lifestyle and start re-offending. But, it could, and certainly nowadays it would, mean a great deal more, as some people discover to their cost and for murder there are statutory starting points from 15 years upwards to 'whole life', i.e. before parole can even be considered.

One of my first serious lessons in the police was when a local 'face', a professional robber, discovered that his wife was being unfaithful to him with another face. He went home to pick up his double-barrelled shotgun, went out to look for his rival, and when he found him blasted him with the shotgun, killing him in front of hundreds of people. The trial was a necessary formality. Despite never having pleaded guilty before, he did so this time and was duly sentenced to life imprisonment. After only five years he secured an appearance before the Parole Board and convinced them of his remorse and that he had changed as a man and would never repeat his crime. He was released under supervision. As he left the prison he was handed a bunch of papers by the principal officer on duty and put his imprisonment behind him as he went for a drink with his mates in order to celebrate his release.

Unfortunately for him, other people had read those papers that he had been given very carefully. They knew that they told every prisoner serving life imprisonment that he could be returned to prison at any time if he committed a crime, or returned to his old habits and started associating with his former criminal associates. The drink-up was, in itself, enough to return him to prison, but the police knew that the Home Secretary might forgive that. They gave him two weeks and followed him as he went round visiting all his old associates. They then prepared a report to the Home Secretary, recording all his meetings. The Home Secretary was convinced, and ordered the prisoner's return to prison. He was now back where he started. He was serving a sentence of life imprisonment and it would be a few more years before he could even apply to appear before the Parole Board and, having been embarrassed by being over-ruled by the Home Secretary, they would be far more cautious about trusting him again. This generated resentment and the prisoner started committing disciplinary offences that added to his sentence and made an appearance before the Parole Board even less likely.

Eventually, he remained in prison for another 20 years. His enemies joked that he received five years for murder and 20 years for 'drinking with his mates'. Roberts had to be careful that this did not happen to him. He appears to have taken the 'old soldier's' course, and kept his head down. He did his time and avoided confrontation with the prison officers. Stories emanating from prison relate that he was held in high esteem by his fellow inmates and many of them appear to have been paying him substantial sums of 'tribute', money for his protection and assistance in intimidating any 'loose cannons' who might threaten them. As a former special forces soldier, Roberts kept himself fit and possessed the skills to deal with any situation that was likely to occur in a prison. The prison staff likewise avoided confrontation with Roberts. Working long hours in order to generate the income that they needed to support their families, eating a poor diet and with few opportunities for exercise, they were no match for Roberts. He started to realise that he could do almost anything that he wanted to.

As Roberts started to settle down and find his way around his new surroundings, his thoughts began to move to ways in which he could escape. He later told a press reporter that for several years after he was gaoled, he thought of nothing else and forced himself to keep fit so that he was always ready to run if the opportunity arose. He also admitted to the press that he had prepared 22 detailed escape plans and that on one occasion his mother was actually caught by prison officers with a pair of bolt cutters in her bra when she went to visit him in prison. On three occasions he was caught and punished for attempting to escape. The one thing that these plans had in common was that he never came close to it.

While in prison, Roberts' wife announced that she was leaving him for a new life. This was only to be expected as few women, however loyal, can be expected to spend their lives waiting for their husbands to complete a 30 year sentence. Roberts did not even have the advantage, like the Great Train Robbers, of leaving their wives comfortably off and able to live the good life. He had a 'spare woman', Lillian Perry, but realising that she too would leave him soon, he decided to accelerate the process and told her to stop visiting him. Fortunately, his mother still visited him.

Roberts remained a Category-A prisoner for 18 years, until 1985 when he was released from the high security block at Gartree Prison and allowed to integrate into the general prison population. He later spoke of his feelings at that time, of being unable to focus his eyes on the end of a corridor, getting lost in the wing because he could not cope with the space, and spending hours staring out of the window of his new cell, looking at fields for the first time in nearly 20 years.

During his time as a Category-A prisoner Roberts would have had no access to radio or newspapers and would have been segregated from the rest of the prisoners, so that he was not able to participate in the prisoners education programme. As soon as he was integrated he undertook O-levels (now GCSEs) in English language and English literature and gained distinctions in two engineering examinations. His success was recognised by the prison authorities when they put him to work in the sock shop, repairing hundreds of pairs of socks belonging to other prisoners. He resented this humiliation and promptly refused to continue working in the sock shop, despite the loss of income. For a while he tried painting, but he gave up as soon as he realised that he was no good at it.

Later Roberts talked to a reporter about what it was like being a hard man in prison, where your fellow prisoners use their considerable free time to study you and see how you are coping with the pressures of prison life. He remembered owning a budgerigar in prison. He had originally got it because he needed the wire from the budgie's cage for an escape attempt that he was planning, but he quickly came to enjoy the bird's company, when all other company was removed. The budgie would sit on his shoulder and he would stroke its beak and feed it breadcrumbs. He told jokes about this bird trying to set up robberies. 'I turned it down. The money he was offering was chickenfeed'. Then the bird died, and that hurt him. 'I could see it was ill. I spent money on a vet. But it died. I nearly cracked up. I'd never have another one. I was really choked and you can't go getting upset in this place'.

A few weeks later, Roberts' mother, Dorothy, died. He later told the press, 'We were very close. Then one day they opened the cell door and said, 'Your mother died yesterday'. Suddenly she's not there anymore. I tried to go to the funeral, but they were talking about a security escort and police outriders and I said, 'This is a circus—forget it'. Someone sent me a couple of photos of the funeral, but they wouldn't let me have 'em. So that's the end of that'.

Roberts was by now 48 years-of-age. He knew things were getting to him one night when he was watching athletics on TV and saw Steve Ovett and Sebastian Coe racing for the finishing line, and he started to cry. Prisoners often say that the system is designed to break their spirit and the truth is that Harry Roberts was all but broken.

Parole

As soon as he had completed 20 years inside, Roberts began asking about parole. What was his tariff? What did he have to do to get paroled? Would it help his case if he volunteered to have a psychiatric examination? What do *you* think that my chances are? He was given a range of answers. He was too big, too strong, too dangerous, still perceived as a threat. He was institutionalised. It didn't take a psychiatrist to see that he still had problems. When he submitted a report asking whether there was a tariff in place in his case, he received a nicely written letter on official headed notepaper a few weeks later informing him that there was a tariff in his case and that another official held it. When he wrote to the named official, he never received a reply. In early 1990, he was told that his case would be considered in July 1992. On the prison grapevine he heard that his co-defendant John Witney had heard the same. He could not find out anything about his other co-defendant, John Duddy.

July passed. Roberts again heard on the grapevine that Witney had been released on parole, but could get no news on his own case. Thinking that the door was ajar if Witney could get parole, he told a reporter, 'So I stuck in a petition to find out the result. It turned out they had cancelled it or never bothered with it. But they hadn't told me that. So then they said they'd review me and give me a result in January 1993. I went ahead and I had this interview with the Lifer Review Committee in November, then another one with the Local Review Committee after Christmas. They said I'd get the result in January. Middle of January, I asked the wing governor where it was. He says 'Oh, we haven't even put the papers in yet. You're not due for anything in January'. 'So what'm I supposed to do?' thought Roberts, 'I'm not lost. I'm trapped'.

He offered to undergo a psychiatric examination at Grendon Underwood, a ground-breaking therapeutic community prison, but was told that he was not considered suitable. He asked how this could be said when he had not been examined for many years. Finally, he told the press, 'They say I should go to church. I ask you. I could do it for six months then I'd have a row with the vicar'.

As 1993 and Roberts' review approached, he gave an interview to the *The Guardian*. The resulting article included the following extracts:

'Justice for men like Harry Roberts has been decided in private by officials of a section of the Prison Department known as DSP2/LSRS. And they don't talk—not about the rules on which they operate, nor about individual cases, not even to the murderers whose fate they are deciding.

When Harry Roberts starts to talk, he seems at first to be as hard now as he was on the day he shot his victims. "They keep asking me 'Do you feel remorse, Harry?' And I say no. We didn't want to murder anyone. That was the last thing we wanted. We shot them because we thought they were going to nick us and we didn't want to go to jail for 15 years. We were professional criminals. We don't react the same way as ordinary people. The police aren't like real people to us. They're strangers, they're the enemy. And you don't feel remorse for killing a stranger. I do feel sorry for what we did to their families. I do. But it's like people I killed in Malaya when I was in the Army. You don't feel remorse."

The hardness has an edge of bravado. Why were they carrying guns that day? "Because we were gangsters." How does he feel each time he arrives at a new prison? "I'm going in there, with my shoulders back, saying 'Right, which one of you lot's done more time than me?'" He chuckles like an indulgent father at the football fans who still chant his name to aggravate policemen—"Harry Roberts, he's our man; he shoots policemen, bang, bang, bang".'

In 2001, he was moved to an open prison. However, Roberts was returned to a closed prison within months after allegations that he was involved in drug dealing and contraband smuggling. Author Kate Kray, who interviewed Roberts for her book *Natural Born Killers*, said that he has no remorse for his victims and recreates the murders in art and pastry decorations, making apple pies and decorating them with pastry cut-outs of policemen being shot. Kray said that he also produces 'precisely drawn and coloured' paintings depicting someone shooting a policeman.

In July 2003, Roberts raised an almost unique case in the High Court. He complained that the Parole Board had declined to allow him to see some of the correspondence on which they decided whether or not to grant him parole. Roberts' solicitor, Simon Creighton, claimed that the reports about Roberts that had been disclosed were 'very positive' but that the failure to disclose other reports meant that Roberts was unable to defend himself against unknown allegations. 'He is struggling to get a fair procedure,' Creighton said. 'You can't have a fair decision about whether someone is to be released if you're not telling them what information you are going to consider as part of your decision'. Creighton said Roberts was being made a 'special case' and normal procedures for dealing with other prisoners had not been followed; 'I think it infringes his human rights'.

Generally, it is a principle of English law that justice should not only be done, but also be seen to be done. Only when there are exceptional risks involved, such as 'national security', will the courts overrule this principal. All previous cases where evidence in a case has not been supplied to a defendant have involved national security. In this case the Parole Board considered the move necessary because of 'the real risk to the physical safety' of the source of the material if it went directly to Roberts or his legal team. Whether that risk was something other than national security in Roberts case can only be the subject of speculation.

The courts attempted to mitigate the disadvantage to the defence by appointing a second barrister, 'a special advocate', who was especially selected by the Parole Board to represent Roberts and who was permitted to see the secret papers, but who was not permitted to speak to Roberts or the barrister who was representing him before the Parole Board, for fear of disclosing any of the confidential material to them. This was a procedure that had evolved in dealing with cases involving national security where the British Government are prosecuting a spy and do not intend to hand over the documents on which they base their case as the prisoner will then deliver them to his employer. Usually, in the past, this has been the former Soviet Union.

The High Court upheld the right of the Parole Board to adopt the 'special advocate' procedure and refused Roberts leave to appeal. Mr Justice Maurice Kay said the procedure was justified in this 'exceptional' case because of the risk of 'inadvertent disclosure' of the sensitive material to Roberts. His solicitor, Simon Creighton, said the judge's ruling meant that the special advocate would represent the prisoner at the secret parole hearing without being allowed to take instructions from him or his lawyers. 'The court has taken an unprecedented step in deciding that the most basic of human rights, the right of a person to know the case they have to answer, no longer exists'. He said Roberts faces the 'bizarre' situation of remaining in prison for the rest of his life 'with no explanation for that decision'. 'He naturally finds it difficult to accept that such a position is tenable in a modern democratic society'.

Roberts, as a Special Forces soldier in Kenya at the time of the Mau Mau Urising and in Malaya at the time of the insurgency there (Aka the Malayan Emergency or Anti-British National Liberation War), might have known something so that he posed a threat to national security. His talk of personally killing four prisoners of war at the instructions of his senior officers, made this a possibility.

On 7 July 2005 Roberts heard that he had lost his appeal to the House of Lords (now the Supreme Court) over the use of secret evidence to keep him in gaol. Lords Bingham, Woolf, Stein, Rodger and Carswell upheld the decision of the Court of Appeal that the use of a special advocate in Roberts' case was not unfair. The evidence had been obtained by tapping private phone calls between Roberts and his solicitor. The material was then introduced as evidence at his parole hearings.

In September 2006, 70-year-old Roberts applied for a judicial review over apparent delays by the Parole Board in reaching a decision to free him by the end of the year. In December 2006, he was again turned down for parole. On 29 June 2007, he was given leave to seek a High Court judicial review over his failed parole bid, with the judge saying his case 'was of great public interest'.

It was reported in February 2009 that Roberts hoped to be freed from prison within months, having already served 42 years in jail and completed the first stage of a Parole Board hearing, he believed this would pave the way for his release. He hoped a final hearing would find that at that age he was no longer a risk to the public and that the Parole Board would order his immediate release. At this time he had already served 12 years more than the minimum term recommended by his trial judge. It was recognised that government Ministers were concerned that any decision on the matter would provoke public fury and that Roberts' personal safety might be put at risk, but if the Home Secretary decided in Roberts' favour, the Parole Board would be powerless to halt the release. A task now the responsibility of the Parole Board and Justice Secretary.

Supporters of Roberts had previously claimed that successive Home Secretaries had blocked his release for political reasons because of fears of a public backlash. However Peter Smyth, chairman of the Metropolitan Police Federation, said that there would be widespread anger among serving and former officers. Legal sources said they believed that the Parole Board was likely to recommend that he was eligible for an open prison as a way of preparing him for his eventual release. Jack Straw, the former Justice Secretary, retained the power to reject a Parole Board recommendation that Roberts be moved to an open prison. However, he could not block a decision by the board to order his release.

In April 2009, the *Mail on Sunday* published an exclusive report. In 2001, Roberts had worked on day release at the St Bernard's Animal Shelter in Chesterfield, Derbyshire, where a Mrs Cartwright and her son secretly complained about his behaviour. He had:

- Boasted of his criminal past and revelled in his notoriety.
- Bought a car and driven up to the gates of his open prison.
- Mixed with violent criminals who treated him like 'a folk hero' and gave him substantial sums of cash.
- Opened a bank account using her son's address.
- Insisted she make him breakfast most mornings — on one occasion flinging a fried egg on her kitchen floor because it wasn't cooked to his liking.
- Claimed prison officers at his open jail were 'in his pocket'.

Roberts knew that a good reference from the animal sanctuary was vital if he was going to be granted parole. After ten months working there, he was abruptly moved to a closed jail, but once there he rang Mrs Cartwright sometimes five times a week, every week for nearly four years. Allegedly, he made threats, and Mrs Cartwright's animals were attacked. In the worst incident, a horse's head was hacked at with an axe the night before she was due to give evidence against him (though there is no definitive attribution of this and similar occurrences to Roberts). On another days after Mrs Cartwright's husband had resisted giving Roberts a character reference another of her horses was attacked and had to be put down. In other assaults between 2002 and 2006, a horse lost an eye after being battered with an iron bar; a donkey died after its pelvis was shattered, probably with a baseball bat; the family's pet cat was electrocuted; and a peacock was strangled.

In 2006 the Parole Board cited his behaviour in 'open conditions' as the reason to refuse parole; and in July 2009, the board determined that Roberts still posed a risk to the public and should continue to serve time, at Littlehey Prison in Cambridgeshire, where he worked in the library.

CHAPTER 12

Roberts' Release

John Duddy

Duddy died at Parkhurst Prison, on the Isle of Wight on 8 February 1981, aged 52.

John Witney

Witney was controversially released on licence from HM Prison Littlehey by Home Secretary Kenneth Baker in 1991, having served 25 years' imprisonment. Baker cravenly surrendered to pressure for his release, on the basis that he had not personally shot any of the victims, ignoring the principle of joint enterprise, that has long been an essential component of English law. It is thought that Witney was the first adult to have been released from a sentence of imprisonment imposed for the murder of a police officer before having completed the term recommended by the trial judge, and questions were asked in Parliament.

On Monday 16 August 1999, 33 years and four days after the Massacre of Braybrook Street, Witney's body was found in a pool of blood in his flat in Horfield, Bristol, apparently after he had been battered to death by a 38-year-old heroin addict who was believed to be his flatmate. A post mortem examination revealed that Witney had suffered horrific head injuries. The accused appeared before Bristol Magistrates' Court charged with murder by Det Ch Insp Mike Hems.

At the time of his death, Witney was on licence and regularly had to report to his probation officer. Witney's neighbours in Bristol had no idea of his terrible secret. One said: 'I expect people around here would have been very worried if they had known'.

Questions were asked in Parliament about Witney's release from prison on 8 July 1991. They were answered by Lord Ferrers, Minister of State at the Home Office. The official record from *Hansard* is set out below:

Mr John Witney: Release from Prison
HL Deb 08 July 1991 vol 530 cc1206–9 1206
2.41 pm

Lord Boyd-Carpenter asked Her Majesty's Government:
Why and on what authority Mr John Witney, who had been sentenced to life imprisonment for participation in the murder of a policeman with a minimum of 30 years' detention prescribed by the trial judge, was released from prison after a substantially shorter period.

The Minister of State, Home Office (Earl Ferrers)
My Lords, Mr Witney was released on life licence after almost 25 years in prison on the authority of my right honourable friend the Home Secretary. This was in exercise of his powers under the Criminal Justice Act 1967 following a recommendation which was made by the Parole Board in 1988 and after consultation with the Lord Chief Justice.

Lord Boyd-Carpenter
My Lords, is my noble friend aware that when sentencing the trial judge said: I think it is likely that no Home Secretary regarding the enormity of your crime will ever think fit to show mercy by releasing you on licence. This is one of the cases in which the sentence of imprisonment for life may well be treated as meaning exactly that"? Is my noble friend also aware that the trial judge felt bound to state a figure for a minimum sentence of 30 years? Will he explain why in those circumstances, and in view of the clear views of the trial judge, the man was released five years before the expiry of those 30 years?

Earl Ferrers
My Lords, I understand my noble friend's anxiety. I remind him that the judge's recommendation is not binding. The detention of life sentence prisoners is determined by the length of time considered necessary to mark the

seriousness of the offence and by the risk which release would present to the public. After consultation with the Lord Chief Justice in 1985 the then Home Secretary decided that a distinction could be drawn between Witney, who did not fire any shots, and the other two co-defendants who did. In November 1988 the Parole Board advised that he no longer presented a risk to the public. That is why in February 1989 my right honourable friend decided that Witney could be released after a further two years.

Phillips, Baroness

My Lords, is the Minister aware that many members of the general public are genuinely disturbed about, first, the light sentences which are being passed; secondly, the fact that some people are not sentenced at all; and thirdly, that people, as this Question shows, are released before the end of their sentence? Is that fair to the police who worked on the case? And is it fair to the rest of us?

Earl Ferrers

My Lords, he was not released before the end of his sentence. He was given a life sentence, and the life sentence continues. The question for the Home Secretary's judgment is how much of that time should be spent in prison. There is anxiety about people who commit these terrible atrocities. I share that anxiety. However, the fact is that my right honourable friend must take advice from the Parole Board. In this case it was considered that Witney was no longer a risk to the public. That is why he was released.

Earl Nelson

My Lords, I should declare an interest in this Question. I was serving in the Metropolitan Police at the time of the murder of three police officers at Shepherd's Bush. One of the officers, Detective Sergeant Christopher Head, was a personal friend of mine.

I am sure that the Minister will be aware of the disappointment which I feel at his Answer. In saying that, I am sure that I speak for every serving police officer in this country. Will the Minister give an assurance that no others who have been sentenced in this way are likely to be granted early release, particularly the third defendant in the case—Harry Roberts—who was also recommended to serve 30 years?

Does the noble Earl agree that there is a certain element of farce, not in the sentencing procedure but in the way in which matters are interpreted in later years? Last week we discussed the Criminal Justice Bill: we heard arguments on both sides. Some people argue that life imprisonment should mean that; others hold different views. However, if sentences are to be overturned, such as in this case, does the Minister not agree that there is a certain element of farce?

Earl Ferrers

My Lords, I appreciate the anxiety of my noble friend Lord Nelson, considering his personal involvement. Understandably, any person who has had such an involvement is more concerned than those of us who have not had such an experience. I regret that my replies have been disappointing to my noble friend. I believe that he means that he is disappointed by the early release of Witney. We must bear in mind that the principle of a life sentence, as it is now determined, is that there should be the possibility of release when a person is considered to be safe for release. It was considered in Witney's case that his participation was different from that of the other two...

With regard to the other people to whom my noble friend referred, every case is considered on its own merits. Roberts remains in closed conditions. The next review of his case will be 1992 but there are no grounds to set aside the trial judge's recommendation. With regard to Witney, his sentence is the equivalent of a determinate sentence of around 36 years.

Lord Monsoon

My Lords, does the noble Earl agree that if the Criminal Justice Bill had already become law and if the other place had not thrown out your Lordships' amendment which abolished the necessity of imposing a mandatory life sentence for murder, the trial judge could have achieved his objective by sentencing Mr Witney to 60 years' imprisonment with the possibility of release after 30 years? If that had happened, there is no way in which he could have been released so soon, except for an urgent medical condition. Therefore, does the Minister agree that those Members of another place who rejected your Lordships' amendment because they wanted to give the impression of being hard on the more heinous forms of murder have shot themselves in the foot?

Earl Ferrers

My Lords, the noble Lord, Lord Monson, carries his imagination rather too far. As regards the Criminal Justice Bill, the changes which may take place—and the Bill is still going through Parliament, so we cannot yet tell what will be changed—will not affect mandatory life sentences as proposed at present.

Lord Boyd-Carpenter

My Lords, can my noble friend confirm that this is the first case in which a man involved in the murder of a policeman has been released on licence? Does that change in policy mean that the Parole Board and the Home Office have altered their policy? Will he be frank about that?

Earl Ferrers

My Lords, I do not believe that the Home Office has altered its policy in the slightest. There have been various occasions when people were released early. Other police killers have been released. Witney is the first adult male convicted of the murder of a policeman since 1965, when the death penalty was abolished, to be released.

Lord Donaldson of Kingbridge

My Lords, one or two people from this side tend to take a different view from that of the noble Lord, Lord Boyd-Carpenter, and those supporting him. Most of us would like to express our view.

Noble Lords

Question!

Lord Donaldson of Kingbridge

My Lords, perhaps I may be allowed to express a view on the matter.

Noble Lords

Order!

Lord Donaldson of Kingbridge

My Lords, I have been doing this for 22 years; I am sorry to have got it wrong. Is the noble Earl aware that some of us believe that 25 years' imprisonment is a long sentence, though in this case not too long? That somebody is released after 25 years on grounds of no longer being a danger to the public is a good reason for releasing him. I do not believe that the noble Earl has exercised any special privileges in that regard.

Earl Ferrers

My Lords, what the noble Lord, Lord Donaldson, says indicates a variety of views …I can only repeat that it is the Home Secretary's duty—and it is an onerous duty—to decide when such a person should be released. He does not release such people lightly …The person concerned has been in prison longer than the minimum recommendations laid down by his former right honourable friend Sir Leon Brittan, when he was Home Secretary. I can only repeat that distressing though this case is …there is a difference between Witney, who did not fire the shots, and the other two who did.

Viscount Mountgarrett

My Lords, does my noble friend agree that while there is considerable sympathy and understanding for those serving long sentences in prison that their cases should be reviewed sympathetically, nonetheless there exists unease in the country as a whole that sometimes too much attention is paid to the miscreant and not enough consideration given to either the victim or possible intended victim? Perhaps the Government will bear that it mind.

Earl Ferrers

My Lords, of course we shall bear that in mind. There is no question that when anyone is murdered, release of the prisoner is a matter of prime concern. When it is the murder of a policeman, that concern is even greater. Only this morning I attended the memorial service of one such policeman who was murdered and it was a distressing occasion.

The Final Release Decisions

On Thursday 23 October 2014, after Roberts had spent nearly 48 years in gaol, the Parole Board announced that they had approved his release, at the age of 78. Having exceeded, by far, his recommended minimum term of 30 years imprisonment, Roberts was, by then, one of the UK's longest-serving prisoners, having remained in custody from 1966 to 2014.

In recent years, the British Government has gone to extraordinary lengths and spent very considerable sums of money on ensuring a safe and equitable release of some people who have served long sentences for serious crimes. Robert Thompson and Jon Venables, who, as boys, murdered two-year-old Jamie Bulger in Liverpool, are just two examples. The release of Harry Roberts presented unprecedented challenges for the authorities charged with monitoring him.

His first months were likely spent under close supervision in a hostel for released prisoners and offenders on bail for a few weeks and where he would be assessed, required to stay in close touch with probation officers and, in the early days at least, keeping his trips out of the hostel simple and advisedly to avoid crowded areas. 'Public protection arrangements' had been put in place to manage Roberts' release: perhaps the Ministry of Justice were concerned that Sir Bernard Hogan-Howe, the (then) Commissioner of Police of the Metropolis would abandon his lifelong vocation to eliminate crime and send his Specialist Firearms Unit round to wreak revenge on Roberts? It is difficult to identify any other potential attacker.

Those on life sentences who are released on parole are subject to strict controls and conditions. If they fail to comply with them they can be immediately returned to prison.

Roberts was released from Littlehey Prison in Cambridgeshire on the evening of Monday 15 November 2014, the 48th anniversary of his arrest in 1966. After his period of assessment he was given a new name to conceal his identity and put in a flat in an old people's home in the South of

England. Several residents in such homes wasted no time in expressing their fury at the fact that his fellow residents would not be informed of the identity of their new neighbour.

Roberts is eligible to receive the basic state pension (of £113 a week at the time of his release), and he may be eligible for housing allowance. But authorities are worried that the public might perceive that one of Britain's most notorious killers was being given special treatment at public expense, and it was made very clear that no additional public funds were being expended on Roberts' release or his life after his release. He was supplied with a panic alarm in case he felt threatened. No details were given of the type of monsters who might be currently roving around the south of England capable of striking fear into the heart of a cop killer.

Reaction to Harry Roberts' Release

The relatives of the deceased detectives

The Wombwell family. Gillian Wombwell with her
late husband, David and their son Daen

Relatives of the police officers slaughtered by Roberts said the killer should remain behind bars for the rest of his life. The distraught widow of one of the hero officers reacted with outrage saying: 'He should die behind bars'. Gillian Wombwell, whose husband David was gunned down by Roberts added: 'Our family has faced life, he should too'. Now

68, she was just 20 years old when widowed and said, 'I was warned he was being released the night before and I'm finding it difficult coping with all my emotions. I'm feeling dreadful. It is incomprehensible. It makes a mockery of the system. He should never be allowed out'. Her son Daen and daughter, Melanie, were just two and three respectively when their father died. She had urged the Parole Board to reject Roberts' latest plea to be released saying, 'They knew my family and the others victims' families never wanted him to get out. I don't understand how they came to this decision'.

'He is a thoroughly evil man who will never adapt to life outside gaol It gives us all great cause for concern. He's an old man now who has spent the last 48 years in an institution. That's all he's ever known for the best part of his life and before that he was a criminal. How is he ever going to adapt and why let him out?'

A retired guest house owner, she saw Roberts seven years ago at a parole hearing and described her feelings: 'It was horrendous, too emotional and too painful. She said, 'I have no interest in what he does and hope that he just hides away'.

Other devastated relatives blasted the decision to free him. 'I feel sick,' said Paul Fox, who was just 16 when his father, Geoffrey was shot dead. 'It's an insult and indignity to all serving police officers that someone can shoot them and go around living their life,' he is quoted as saying. Then 64-years-of-age and living in Aylesbury in Buckinghamshire, he added: 'My family has been totally destroyed. ... It is something I live with on a daily basis — that face is ingrained in my head ... I was hoping this day would never come. I found out about it watching TV ... I thought they were supposed to consider the victims and give us a say on if he should be released. At the very least I should have had a phone call'.

Blasting the Parole Board for failing to put victims first Paul Fox added: 'I was always surprised that none of the officers received any kind of posthumous medal or anything that recognised their bravery. They were protecting the public'. Paul's sister Mandy added: 'What signal does this show our courageous police officers who put their lives on the line daily for our protection and safety?'

Speaking in the House of Commons Labour MP Ian Austin said: 'People out there are absolutely furious ... Home Secretary Theresa May promised the country life should mean life for anybody convicted of killing a police officer'. Under new laws proposed this year, 2014, future police killers will never be released under compulsory whole-life terms. She also said that she believed that sentence handed to Roberts was not enough, but attempted to distance herself from the decision to release Roberts, realising that it was a high-profile case that would arouse public fury and ridicule her lack of action to implement her public policy. She insisted that the decision had been made by the Independent Parole Board and was beyond the control of the government and stressed that the law was being reviewed to ensure that future police killers will remain behind bars for the rest of their lives.

Kate Kray, the widow of Ronnie Kray, interviewed Roberts for her book *Natural Born Killers*. In it she says that Roberts had no remorse for his victims and recreates the murders in art and pastry decorations, making apple pies and decorating them with cut-outs of policemen being shot. She also claims that he produces 'precisely drawn and coloured' paintings depicting someone shooting a policeman.

The police

Many police officers were left furious after learning that Roberts may soon be freed, especially as the decision came only a year after then Home Secretary (and now Prime Minister) Theresa May vowed to make sure that 'life means life' for police killers.

Former Metropolitan Police Commissioner Sir Bernard Hogan-Howe said: 'The murdered officers in 1966 were unarmed and doing their duty on behalf of society. 'Officers of both yesterday and today deserve the full protection of the law when facing ruthless criminals and in this case 'life' should have meant what it said'.

Another former Commissioner of the Metropolitan Police, Lord Stevens said Roberts should not be released from gaol. 'The impact of this terrible crime was horrendous', he said. 'This is a case where life imprisonment should mean exactly that—life'.

Steve White, chairman of the Police Federation of England and Wales, the body which represents police officers, said: 'Police officers up and down the country will be absolutely furious and disgusted that Harry Roberts has been released. I am appalled to learn that police killer Harry Roberts is being released from prison. This menace murdered three unarmed officers in cold blood. This decision by the parole board is a slap in the face for the families of the three police officers he brutally murdered who, once again, are forced to re-live their pain and loss. It will spark fury among everyone in the police family who will feel badly let down. The judge said Roberts should never be released—that has just been forgotten and thrown in the bin. This is a betrayal of the police officers who died. It is abhorrent news'.

He said he had written to then Home Secretary Theresa May asking her to keep her promise to ensure whole life sentences are given to people who kill police officers—though subsequent legislation and guidelines will not apply to criminals who have already been sentenced.

John Tully, chairman of the Metropolitan Police branch of the Police Federation has described Roberts' release as 'sickening'.

Politicians

Immediately after the shootings and at the height of the public outrage at the crime, the then Home Secretary, Roy Jenkins described the killings as 'a threat to the whole fabric of society'.

In sharp contrast, 50 years later, the then leader of the Liberal party, Deputy Prime Minister Nick Clegg defended the decision to free Roberts, saying, 'If you want to run the system according to the latest emotion you feel, fine, but that would be a disaster. Such a decision is not about 'feelings' but 'how the justice system works'.

Theresa May and the then London Mayor (and later Foreign Secretary) Boris Johnson, who shared a responsibility for policing in London, joined in calling for Roberts to remain behind bars.

The trial judge

At the end of the trial in 1966 Sir Hildreth Glyn-Jones sentenced Roberts and his co-defendants to life imprisonment and set a tariff of thirty years imprisonment for each of the defendants. He commented that the murders were 'the most heinous crime to have been committed in this country for a generation or more'.

The death penalty had been removed for offences of murder just eight months before the shootings in Shepherd's Bush. The Judge's daughter, Anne, spoke to the press after Roberts release from gaol in 2014. She told them that her father 'wanted to hang him for his crimes instead'. Ms Glyn-Jones, 91 at the time of Roberts' release, attended the trial of Roberts and his two fellow defendants in 1966. She said that her father would not have wanted him to be released:

'If the death penalty had been in force he would have given it to them with no reservation and he would have been very surprised to see him being released today...He thought Roberts knew exactly what he was doing when he killed those men and should not be released and said as much at the time. He thought he was a very evil man...While he did not enjoy passing out death sentences my father was a great supporter of the police and like many others at the time was unhappy about the removal of this protection. His view was that the police are so much more exposed than anyone else and they put their lives on the line and should be protected. He had delivered many death sentences and while he felt unhappy at sending, for example, a poisoner to her death he did not feel that way about police killers. If the death penalty had been in force he would have given it to them with no reservation.

My father presided over the trial of some prison guards at Mauthausen concentration camp. He sentenced 12 to death and with one of them I know he felt there were extenuating circumstances. He went to see the boss of the control commission in Austria about it and tried to get the death sentence he passed commuted but it was refused. It is not something he would have done in the case of Roberts and the others—he thought them very evil men.'

Recalling the trial she said:

'I went with some friends…My boss gave me some time off so I could attend and I was able to get a privileged seat inside the court room…The trial started with only two of them and then midway through Roberts was found camping in Epping Forest and [he] had to make the difficult decision to continue with him not start again. It's been a long time but I remember some details. Harry Roberts was I think a sergeant in Malaya and a very good one I recall. I recall him being very brazen: he stood in the dock looking around catching the eye of any females.

His hands were on the front of the dock and I was very riveted by them. They had beautiful sensitive long fingers, not what you would have expected of a Malayan jungle sergeant. The person next to me at the trial asked me if I had noticed them and they were very unexpected. They were very elegant and could have been the hands of an artist. There was a charisma about him; he was leader who inspired a certain amount of admiration despite what he had done. My father didn't think that Roberts was at the bottom of it all but he was certainly aware of what he was doing.'

The latest woman in Roberts life

A 50-year-old grandmother took advantage of Roberts' release to announce to the national press that she had enjoyed a three-year relationship with Roberts while he was behind bars. She revealed she had been swept away by the 'charming' Roberts. As there is no record of Roberts being released, even briefly, in that period, there was no opportunity for them to touch or become intimate.

She claimed that she had written to him in July 2010 when she read about his case and thought he deserved to be freed. Since then she claimed that they had exchanged dozens of love letters (all presumably strictly censored by prison staff) and that he had expressed a desire to set up home with her when he got out. She also claimed that Roberts had even admitted regret over the murders; but this appears to be nothing more than a wish that he had not spent most of his life in gaol. Apparently he had told her: 'I think about it every night I lay on my bed. I wish I hadn't done it because I wouldn't be in here'. She says she 'eventually came to her senses' and dumped him in 2013 and broke his heart.

CHAPTER 13

Epilogue: Meeting Harry Roberts

In 2014, Home Secretary (and future Prime Minister) Teresa May made a major public statement in which she declared that, in future, for all police killers life would mean life and that anybody killing a police officer should expect to die in gaol. It therefore came as a great surprise when, less than a week later, the same Teresa May announced that she had accepted a Parole Board recommendation to release the worst police killer in British history, Harry Roberts.

The release of a man who was by then 78-years-old and had spent almost 48 years of his life not only in prison but in solitary confinement, would clearly present problems. Despite his age, Roberts was extremely fit. He had been a special services soldier in Malaya and since then he had spent his life eating a calorie-controlled, balanced diet and exercising twice a day. He had gone to bed every night at 10 pm, never smoked, drunk or, according to prison officers, indulged in any sort of sexual activity.

The psychological health of a man who can suddenly explode and kill three policemen in cold blood must be a source of some concern. Forty years the majority of that time held in solitary confinement is unlikely to improve that condition. Neither is a sudden change of environment, to a life with which he is unfamiliar. Life in 1966 when Roberts went to prison was completely different to life in 2005 when he came out. In 1960 the average weekly wage was just £14, and there were only a quarter of a million unemployed people in the country. It was in 1966 that the government announced that all houses had electricity. The first hand-held calculators and colour televisions were introduced, although there were only 20,000 computers in the world, probably as each one cost the equivalent of £67,000 in today's money. There were certainly no laptops, iPads or mobile telephones.

As a prisoner sentenced to life imprisonment, Roberts will remain on licence until he dies. He will be subject to directions on where and how he lives, what he does and who he associates with. Any breach of those directions could result in his being immediately returned to prison on the signature of any one of her Majesty's Principal Secretaries of State, without trial or review and he would then remain in prison until he died or until his case was again reviewed by the Parole Board.

At the time that the decision was made to release him he was being detained in HM Prison Littlehey in Cambridgeshire. The prison was built on the site of a former borstal where Roberts had been detained as a boy, so he must have known the area well. Arrangements were made for him to be moved upon his release to a half-way house in Peterborough some 28 miles away. As Peterborough had lost its own serial killer just a few months earlier when Joanna Dennehy had been convicted and sentenced to life imprisonment for (seducing and) murdering a number of old men, they appear to have been allocated an equally notorious killer when Harry Roberts arrived there.

Arrangements for Roberts' started even before the decision to release him was made, including a suitable half-way house to accommodate him. Changes were made to the entrance way and exits to improve security. The building accommodates around 100 residents and has a frontage onto the main road on two sides. Thick, heavy blast proof curtains and nets were fitted to all windows on the ground and first floors to prevent any view into the premises. A number of the residents were moved away in order to make space for Roberts and to avoid any potential conflict with him that might lead to violence. Several new, younger, stronger members of staff were introduced to replace older, less active members. Residents that I spoke to told me that they had been called together for several meetings to be told of Roberts' impending arrival, the changes to the regime and that they must not speak to anybody about his arrival or his presence in the home. Arrangements were made for a minibus to take him to and from the home, invariably on the floor of the bus and covered by a blanket.

Quickly Roberts fell into a regular pattern of living. He rose before 6 am, washed and dressed, snatched a quick breakfast and was driven out of the home on the floor of the minibus and dropped off a few hundred yards away, out of sight of the home, where nobody would recognise him. He would then jog the six miles to a new purpose-built gymnasium, where the other users appeared to share an interest in black Hummers, and he could be seen through the windows training hard and lifting exceptional weights for a man of his age.

Around 12 noon he could be seen leaving the gym and crossing the main road to catch a bus back into Peterborough, where he visited the same town centre supermarket in order to buy his lunch and retire to a park behind it to consume his food. He frequently wore Oakley sunglasses, even in poor weather, presumably in order to conceal the prominent eyes and brow that might well reveal his identify to any concerned local residents. When he had finished eating, he would return to the area of the home and use a telephone box and await the minibus collecting him and returning him to it. He seldom went out again that day.

I went to Peterborough several times and saw him maintain this regular routine. Occasionally he would walk through his local shops, past the bank and the local tropical fish and reptile shop. On one occasion I followed him onto the bus as he left the gym. After a couple of minutes I moved to sit next to him. He looked me in the eye but said nothing.

'Good afternoon,' I said.

He replied, 'Fuck off'.

'I know who you are and I would like to speak to you for a minute'.

'Fuck off,' he repeated.

I said, 'Sir, you are still on licence. A confrontation here would be enough to send you back from whence you came. Why not listen to me for just a minute and I will be off. You might hear something that interests you'. Roberts remained silent.

I said, 'I work in the media. I have access to newspapers, radio and TV and can get your message out in any of these. This is my number and this is my email. Think about it and get back to me and I will come back and see you again'.

I dropped the sheet of paper in his lap and got off the bus. He never did get back to me.

Since his release, he has maintained a regular presence in the press. There are tales that he had passed his driving test. On 23 April 2016 the *Daily Mirror* alleged that Roberts was selling signed mug shots of himself on Gangsterstuff.com for £100 a time. *The Star* claims that he told one of its reporters, 'I'll fucking smash you'.

Conclusion

Only time will tell if the story of 'Harry Roberts, Foxtrot One-One and the Shepherd's Bush Massacre' ends here and whether Roberts, already approaching his 80th birthday, lives a long life, or whether he will take out the list of 50 names that he reputedly maintained and updated whilst in prison of people who have wronged him and on whom it has been said he plans to seek revenge. Perhaps the final chapter is still to be written.

Roberts has never expressed what could be considered real remorse for his actions in killing the police officers, attempting instead to confuse ignorant and naïve people with claims of regret for the total of 55 years that he has spent behind bars for all the crimes of which he was convicted over his lifetime.

It is interesting that a week after Roberts' release, the newspapers claimed that the late Mad Frankie Fraser the 'enforcer' for the Kray and Richardson gangs in the 1950s, 1960s and 1970s spent almost half of his life in prison, but nobody yet has mentioned that Harry Roberts spent a great deal more than that behind bars. So far, more than 70 per cent of his life. Fraser was known as 'The Dentist' due to his penchant for removing the teeth of his enemies with pliers; he also used to apply electricity to their testicles using a dynamo, and to maintain the dynamo he used the same tool. Subject to ratification, Roberts's achievement is very likely to be a British record, but not one aspired to by many people.

Several branches of the media have expressed an interest in speaking to Roberts and hearing his story. There can be little doubt that he has no shame and a large ego and that he would likely enjoy the publicity if he were to talk about his life, which he has almost completely wasted along with the lives of his unfortunate victims.

Index

A

Acton *70*

Acton, Det Sgt Sheila *65*

alibi *70*

Antoniades, Achilles *101*

appeal *164*

armed criminals *xiii*

Ashbridge, Reverend John *35*

assault with intent to rob *109*

Attorney-General *148*

Austin, Ian MP *186*

Avon and Somerset Police *104*

B

'bag carrier' *59*

Bailey, Bill *58*

Baker, Kenneth *177*

ballistics *74*

Baron, Cyril *33*

Beaumont Arms *26*

Begg, Det Sgt *61*

Bentley, Derek *124*

Berry, Det Sgt Robert *65*

Bethnal Green *142*

Biggs, Ronald *83*

Bingham, Lord *173*

Bishops Stortford *86, 157*

black market *108*

Blake, George *23, 92, 140, 144–146, 165*

body armour *40*

bolt cutters *168*

bookmaking *116, 120, 143*

borstal *109*

Bourke, Sean *140, 145*

Bow Street Magistrates' Court *98*

Boyd-Carpenter, Lord *178*

Bradbury, Det Supt Sidney *116*

bragging *89*

bravado *93*

bravery *35*

Braybrook Street *19, 139, 151*

   Massacre of Braybrook Street *ii, 15*

bread and water *118*

Brentford *55*

bricklaying *117*

Bridego Bridge *123*

Bristol *104, 115, 125, 177*

   Bristol Crown Court *104*

   Bristol Magistrates' Court *177*

Brown, Det Ch Insp Bob *80, 151*

brutality *37*

budgerigar *169*

Bulger, James *183*

bullets *67*

bullying *120, 143*

Burge, James *163*

Butler, Det Ch Supt Tommy *58*
Butlin, Billy *42*

C

Camberwell *143*
Camden Town *96–97*
camping equipment *157*
capital punishment *38, 123, 166, 188*
'Carl' *119*
car registration number *68*
Cartwright, Mrs *174*
Catholicism *109*
chant (about Roberts) *17*
charges *77*
Charlton, Bobby *69, 70, 103, 152*
Chesterfield *174*
children *20, 69*
Chiswick *55*
  Chiswick Cemetery *35*
  Chiswick Police Station *57*
Chitty, Det Supt Richard *33, 57–58, 70, 152, 160*
Christie, John *123*
City and Guilds *117*
Clegg, Nick MP *187*
clues *68, 139*
common purpose *163*
Comyn, James *154*
Coote, Det Insp Kenneth *24, 64*
cordon *87*
coroner *15, 32–33*
corruption *64*
Costas, Christos *97*
Court of Appeal *164*
Craig, Christopher *124*

Creighton, Simon *172*
Criminal Investigation Department *21*
Criminal Records Office *74*
Croydon *124*
Cunningham, John *86, 157*

D

daily briefing *26, 64*
Daily Mirror *78*
Daimler *115, 156*
dangerous duty *xiii*
Deacon, Bryan *68*
death penalty. See *capital punishment*
Defector's Weld *26*
Dennehy, Joanna *192*
Dent, DC Alistair *29*
Dick, Cressida *x*
Director of Public Prosecutions *157*
Donaldson, Lord *181*
drawings *114*
driving licence *160*
drugs *171*
Du Cane Road *ii, 140*
Duddy, John *15, 78, 103–106, 136*
Duddy, Vincent *80*
Du Rose, John *34, 55*

E

Ealing *55*
East Acton *23*
education *169*
Elephant and Castle *125*
Ellis, Ruth *123*
enterprise *177*
Epping *156*

Epping Forest *84*

Erconwald Street *68*

escape *140*, *168*

Essex

Essex Police *87*

Essex Quarter Sessions *110*

Evans, Nigel *104*

Evans, Timothy *123*

evidence *28*

circumstantial evidence *76*

Queen's evidence *137*

secret evidence *173*

exhibits *62*

F

fairness *172*

false trail *85*

F District *53–56*

F-Division *25*, *30*, *64*

Ferrers, Lord *178*

fingerprints *73*, *87*

Fingerprint Branch *62*

firearms *16*, *125*, *160*. See also *guns*

Metropolitan Police Firearms Unit *xiii*

police use of *39*

Flying Squad *15*, *58*, *111*

Foot, Dingle *155*, *163*

forensics *28*, *62*, *69*

forensic examination of crime scene *67*

'forensic quarantine' *74*

forgery *158*

Fosbury, Det Sgt Ted *59*

Fox, Geoffrey *15*, *19*, *49*, *67*

Fox, Margaret *31*

Foxtrot One-One *24*, *139*, *145*

frame *59*

Fraser, Frankie *194*

Freeman, Leonard *34*

French *142*

Fulham. See *Hammersmith and Fulham*

funeral *34*

G

gangs/gangsters *16*, *53*, *143*, *162*, *171*

Garbut, Sgt George *72*

Gartree Prison *168*

Gaynes Hall Borstal *109*

Gladstone bag *59*

Glasgow *80*, *105*

Glyn-Jones, Mr Justice *147*

Glyn-Jones, Sir Hildreth *188*

Goodall, Det Ch Insp Tom *81*

Goodchild, Rt Reverend *35*

Grant, Thomas *140*

Great Train Robbery *22*, *62*, *83*, *116*, *164*

Grendon Underwood *170*

guns *41*, *90*, *96*, *114*. See also *firearms*

Luger pistol *20*, *156*

Webley revolver *xiii*, *20*

H

Hair, Gilbert *117*

half-way house *192*

Hammersmith and Fulham *53*

Hammersmith Coroner's Court *33*

Hammersmith Hospital *140*

Hammersmith nudes murders *55*

Hammersmith Police Station *61*

Hampstead Heath *90*

Harrods bombing *22*

Head, Christopher *15, 19, 45, 55, 67*

Head, Phyllis *30*

Heath, Edward *36*

Hems, Det Ch Insp Mike *104, 177*

'Henderson, Sammy' *71*

Hensley, Det Ch Insp John (Ginger) *57, 61, 77*

Heron Trading Estate *55*

Hertfordshire Constabulary *87*

High Court *171, 172*

Hilton of Upton, Lord *37*

Hogan-Howe, Bernard *183*

Hogan-Howe, Sir Bernard *186*

Holbrook, Frederick *114*

Home Office pathologist *29, 66*

Home Secretary *29, 36, 164, 174, 186*

Homicide Act **1957** *124*

homosexuality *112*

Horan, PC Bernard *35*

Horfield, Bristol *177*

Horn Lane, Birmingham *160*

House of Lords *173*

Howard, Colin *106, 110, 157–160*

Howard, June *86, 106, 133–138, 156*

Hudson, Mr W M *153–154, 158–163*

human rights *172*

I

identity parade *75*

imprisonment *110*

Incident Room *59*

indictment *148*

inquest *33*

investigation *67–102*

    investigating officer *61*

Ireland, Mungo *55*

J

Jenkins, Roy MP *xiii, 36, 187*

Johnson, Boris (Mayor of London) *187*

joint enterprise *103*

Jones, Det Insp Peter *83*

Jones, Elwyn *148*

judicial review *173*

K

Kay, Mr Justice *172*

Kennington *160*

Kenya *109*

KGB *145*

Knight, Det Supt *48*

knives *121*

Kray Brothers *142, 186*

Kray, Kate *171, 186*

L

Ladbroke Grove *78*

Lawrence, Ronald *65*

life imprisonment *104, 165–176*

Little Cyprus *97*

Littlehey Prison *175, 177, 183, 192*

Liverpool *183*

M

Maida Vale *78*

    Wymering Mansions *133*

Maidstone Prison *110*

Malaya *109, 166, 173*

Mark, Sir Robert *64*

Martin, DC Clive *65*

Martin, Joseph *114*, *116*

Marylebone Magistrates' Court *24*, *27*, *64*, *146*

Mathams Wood *88*

Mathew, John *101*, *153*

Maude, Mr Justice *111*

May, Teresa *191*

May, Theresa MP *186*

McCafferty, John *74*

McCormack, Tommy *69*

McVicar, John *109*

media/press *29*, *78*, *194*

memorial
  memorial service *35*
  Police Memorial Trust *43*

Metropolitan Police Federation *174*

Miles, PC Sidney *124*

Millen, Commander Ernie *57*

Mills, Freddie *55*

Monsoon, Lord *180*

mortuary *29*

motive *139*

Mountgarrett, Viscount *182*

murder *55*
  Murder (Abolition of Death Penalty) Act *125*
  Murder Squad *57*

museum
  Metropolitan Police Crime Museum *x*

N

National Service *109*

Nelson, Earl *179*

Newton, Jimmy *69*

number plates *74*

O

O'Brien, *159*

Official Secrets Act 1911 *144*

O'Hara, Bridget *55*

Old Bailey *96*, *124*, *140*, *142*, *144–146*, *147*

Old Oak Common Housing Estate *20*, *140*

Old Oak Primary School *20*

open prison *174*

Owen, PC David *68*

P

Paddington *136*

Parker, Lord Chief Justice *144*

Parkhurst Prison *99*, *106*, *177*

Parliament *178*

parole *16*, *123*, *166*, *170*
  Parole Board *185*

Perry, Lillian *86*, *96*, *114*, *133–138*, *156*

Peterborough *192*

Philo, Alfred *115*

photographs *29*

plumbing *117*

'POETS Day' *69*

police. See also *F District*; See also *F-Division*
  armed police *84*
  Police Dependants' Fund/Trust *38–42*, *41*, *91*
  Stolen Car Squad *48*

premonition *30*

Prime Minister *29*, *36*

priorities *29*

prison
  life imprisonment *186*, *188*

prison break *64*

prison officers *20, 38, 108, 114, 118, 166,*
　　　167, 168, 174, 191

segregation *168*

trusty *117*

prostitute killing spree *55*

Putney Police Station *59*

Q

Q-car *21, 38, 64*

R

radio *41, 84*

　radio car *21*

rationing *108*

receiving stolen property *77, 108*

rehabilitation *112, 117*

release *177–190*

remorse *167.* See also *Roberts, Harry: lack*
　　　of regret/remorse

rent collectors *22*

Republic of Ireland *92*

Richardson Brothers *143*

Richardson, Kenneth *155*

Rifle Brigade *109*

Rillington Place *123*

robbery *16, 22, 85, 105, 111*

　Great Train Robbery *123*

　United Dairies Robbery *115*

Roberts, Dorothy *84, 108, 128–133*

Roberts, Harry *15, 107–126.* See also *chant*
　　　(about Roberts); See also *women:*
　　　in Roberts' life; See also *Wormwood*
　　　Scrubs Prison: Roberts in

　Army deserter *132*

arrest of *86*

boyhood *127*

building trade *134*

deviant artwork *186*

hard man/tough guy *166, 169*

imprisonment *127, 188*

Kenya *127*

lack of regret/remorse *16, 93, 171, 194*

Malaya *127*

'nutcase' *126*

paintings *114*

release *177–190*

Roberts today *191–194*

'Robin' *131*

school expulsion *109*

schooling *127*

search for *83*

special forces soldier *168*

story teller *122*

survival skills *83*

tent, etc. *86*

wife-beating *122*

Roberts, Harry Snr *108*

Roberts, Margaret *85*

Russell Hotel *156*

S

Sawbridgeworth *155*

Scotland Yard *21, 82*

Seager, PC Sidney *21*

search *97*

　fingertip search *67*

Seaton, R E *100*

security *169*

　high security *168*

national security *172*

security guard *68*

self-defence *xiii*

serial killer *55*

Shepherd's Bush *19*

Shepherd's Bush Massacre/Murders *15, 57*

Shepherd's Bush Police Station *21*

Simpson, Sir Joseph *34, 37*

Slipper, Det Insp Jack *22, 62, 70, 131, 151, 159*

Smith, Mrs *104*

Smith, Sgt Peter *88*

Smyth, Peter *174*

'snout' *116*

soft targets *22*

Solicitor-General *155*

solitary confinement *191*

special advocate *172*

Special Forces *166*

spieler *97*

Squires, Det Supt *62*

Standard Vanguard *15, 20, 160*

St Bernard's Animal Shelter *174*

Stevens, Lord *186*

Steventon, Det Insp Ronald *64, 69*

St Joseph's Academy *129*

St Joseph's College, West Norwood *109*

Stoke Newington *111*

store-breaking *110*

Straw Jack *174*

surgeon *29*

surveillance *ix, 84*

T

tariff *170*

Teare, Dr Donald *66*

terrorism

Anti-Terrorist Branch *15*

'The Dentist' *194*

theft *110*

This Is Your Life *108*

Thompson, Edith *123*

Thompson, Robert *183*

Thorley Hall *157*

Thorley Wood *86, 89, 156*

Tinworth Street *162*

torture *143*

trial *147, 189*

Tully, John *187*

Turnham Green *78*

V

Vale, Edward *78*

Vauxhall *152*

Venables, Jon *183*

Vibart, Det Supt Peter *58*

victims *67, 138, 184–186, 194*

violence *40, 113, 121, 143, 192*

W

Wanstead *108*

West London Magistrates' Court *25, 33, 155*

Westminster Abbey *36*

Weston-Super-Mare *114*

widows *30*

Wilson, Harold *36*

Winner, Sir Michael *43*

witnesses *67*

Witney, John *15, 70, 103–105, 108, 151, 160, 177*

Wombwell, David *15, 19, 48, 67*

Wombwell, Gillian *32, 184*

women

in Roberts' life *84–88*

women police constables *84*

Wood Green *115*

World Cup *19*

Wormwood Scrubs Prison *15, 20, 56*

Roberts in *112, 127*

Wymering Mansions *156*

Y

Yahuda, Joseph *100*

Yeading Green *31*

Z

Zec, Donald *36*

The Tottenham Outrage and Walthamstow Tram Chase
The Most Spectacular Hot Pursuit in History
by Geoffrey Barton. With a Foreword by Mike Waldren QPM.

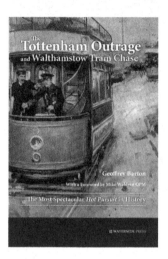

Not since the days of highwaymen and footpads had armed robbery been seen in London. Geoffrey Barton explains the political backdrop to the arrival in the UK of armed revolutionaries driven by their own frenzied missions, causing citizens to go in fear. Laws were passed to deal with aliens and terrorism but as the author explains the civil police were ill-equipped to deal with the problem. Although well known to local people, the Tottenham Outrage of 1909 when two Latvian robbers, Jewish refugees, intercepted a payroll has been comparatively hidden to the wider world (unlike the notorious Siege of Sydney Street which took place two years later). Resulting in the most spectacular police pursuit in history it involved a hundred police officers and up to a thousand citizens in running to ground two desperate police killers. The book follows every inch of the six-and-a-half miles and minute of the two-and-a-half hours of the chase. It also pays minute attention to the people and places involved as well as the aftermath.

Paperback & eBook | ISBN 978-1-909976-40-5 | 2017 | 224 pages

Lizzie Borden and the Massachusetts Axe Murders
by Ronald Bartle

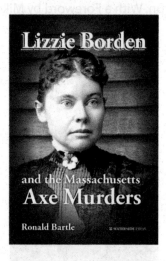

The case of Lizzie Bordon is one of the most infamous in criminal history having spawned songs, plays and a range of publications. It also ranks as one of the most puzzling. Having been acquitted of the axe murders of both her parents, Borden then simply returned home and carried on as before only to be roundly ostracised by the stoutly religious local community. Prosecutors never charged anyone else with the crimes leaving the case naggingly unsolved. Here, author Ronald Bartle revisits the events which occurred in Fall River, Massachussets in 1892. He explains how her answers to police questions were at times strange and contradictory and her accounts to them often bizarre. With so many pointers to her involvement the trial has been compared to that of O J Simpson in the modern day.

Paperback & eBook | ISBN 978-1-909976-43-6 | 2017 | 256 pages

www.WatersidePress.co.uk

The Killing of Constable Keith Blakelock
The Broadwater Farm Riot
by Tony Moore. With a Foreword by Clive Emsley.

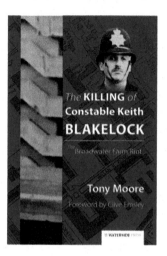

A closely observed account by someone working at senior level in the Met at the time. Deals with the biggest breakdown in community relations and law and order in modern English social and policing history. Looks at the entire sequence of events from their first rumblings to their aftermath and legacy. The murder of PC Keith Blakelock during rioting on the Broadwater Farm Estate, Tottenham, came against a backdrop of unrest in major UK cities and nadir in relations between police and black communities. After becoming detached from Serial 502 Keith Blakelock was kicked and hacked to death by a mob using clubs, iron bars, knives and a machete or similar weapon. His killers have never been brought to justice.

'This is a remarkable book… it is not for the faint-hearted and anyone who has policed in such dire circumstances may well be moved to tears. It should be compulsory reading not only for public order trainers and commanders but all senior officers. It is highly recommended'— *Police History Society newsletter.*

Paperback & eBook | ISBN 978-1-909976-40-5 | 2017 | 224 pages